W9-BRN-815

HINDUISM, TM AND HARE KRISHNA

Zondervan
Guide to Cults &
Religious Movements

ZONDERVAN
GUIDE to CULTS &
RELIGIOUS
MOVEMENTS

HINDUISM, TM AND HARE KRISHNA

J. ISAMU YAMAMOTO
Author

Alan W. Gomes
Series Editor

ZondervanPublishingHouse
Grand Rapids, Michigan

A Division of HarperCollins*Publishers*

To my son, Jeffrey

Hinduism, TM and Hare Krishna
Copyright © 1998 by J. Isamu Yamamoto

Requests for information should be addressed to:

ZondervanPublishingHouse
Grand Rapids, Michigan 49530

Library of Congress Cataloging-in-Publication Data

Yamamoto, J. Isamu.
    Hinduism, TM and Hare Krishna / J. Isamu Yamamoto.
        p.   cm. — (Zondervan guide to cults and religious movements)
    ISBN: 0-310-70391-3 (softcover)
    1. Hinduism. 2. Transcendental Meditation. 3. International Association
for Krishna Consciousness. 4. Hinduism—Relations—Christianity 5.
Christianity and other religions—Hinduism. I. Title. II. Series. III. Series:
Zondervan guide to cults & religious movements.
    BL1205.Y36   1998
    261.2'45—dc21   97-50218
                                                  CIP

All Scripture quotations, unless otherwise indicated, are taken from the *Holy Bible: New International Version*®. NIV®. Copyright © 1973, 1978, 1984 by International Bible Society. Used by permission of Zondervan Publishing House. All rights reserved.

All rights reserved. No part of this publication may be reproduced, stored in a retrieval system, or transmitted in any form or by any means—electronic, mechanical, photocopy, recording, or any other—except for brief quotations in printed reviews, without the prior permission of the publisher.

Interior design by Art Jacobs

Printed in the United States of America

98 99 00 01 02 03 04 05 /❖ DP/ 10 9 8 7 6 5 4 3 2 1

 Contents

How to Use This Book

The *Zondervan Guide to Cults and Religious Movements* comprises fifteen volumes, treating many of the most important groups and belief systems confronting the Christian church today. This series distills the most important facts about each and presents a well-reasoned, cogent Christian response. The authors in this series are highly qualified, well-respected professional Christian apologists with considerable expertise on their topics.

We have designed the structure and layout to help you find the information you need as quickly as possible. All the volumes are written in outline form, which allows us to pack substantial content into a short book. With some exceptions, each book contains, first, an introduction to the cult, movement, or belief system. The introduction gives a brief history of the group, its organizational structure, and vital statistics such as membership. Second, the theology section is arranged by doctrinal topic, such as God, Christ, sin, and salvation. The movement's position is set forth objectively, primarily from its own official writings. The group's teachings are then refuted point by point, followed by an affirmative presentation of what the Bible says about the doctrine. The third section is a discussion of witnessing tips. While each witnessing encounter must be handled individually and sensitively, this section provides some helpful general guidelines, including both dos and don'ts. The fourth section contains annotated bibliographies, listing works by the groups themselves and books written by Christians in response. Fifth, each book has a parallel comparison chart, with direct quotations from the group's literature in the left column and the biblical refutation on the right. Some of the books conclude with a glossary.

One potential problem with a detailed outline is that it is easy to lose one's place in the overall structure. Therefore, we have provided graphical "signposts" at the top of the odd-numbered pages. Functioning like a "you are here" map in a shopping mall, these graphics show your place in the outline, including the sections that come before and after your current position. (Those familiar with modern computer software will note immediately the resemblance to a "drop-down" menu bar, where the second-level choices vary depending on the currently selected main menu item.) In the theology section we have also used "icons" in the margins to make clear at a glance whether the material is being presented from the group's viewpoint or the Christian viewpoint. For example, in the Mormonism volume the sections presenting the Mormon position are indicated with a picture resembling the angel Moroni in the margin; the biblical view is shown by a drawing of the Bible.

We hope you will find these books useful as you seek "to give an answer to everyone who asks you to give the reason for the hope that you have" (1 Peter 3:15).

—Alan W. Gomes, Ph.D.
Series Editor

 Part I:
Introduction

I. Historical Background (Ancient)

A. Hinduism as It Relates to India
  1. *Hindu* is a Persian term that means "the people and culture of the Indus River region."
     a. The Indus River runs from the Himalayas to the Arabian Sea through Pakistan.
     b. The Indus River region includes Pakistan and western India.
     c. In time the term has come to commonly refer to the majority of the Indian population.
  2. Hinduism is more than just a religious term to Indian Hindus.
     a. To them it is more a way of life than a set of beliefs.
     b. According to Sarvepalli Radhakrishnan, a former Indian president and one of the leading Indian philosophers, "Hinduism is more a culture than a creed."[1]
  3. A knowledge of the cultural history of India is imperative in understanding Hinduism.
     a. Yet it also should be noted that Indian scholarship has not been concerned with chronology.
     b. Hence, the lack of reliable historical data handicaps an exact examination of the development of their religious philosophies.

B. The Harappan Civilization
  1. Archaeological artifacts indicate that the Harappan civilization, also known as the Indus Valley civilization, probably thrived from about 2700 to 1750 B.C.
     a. Contemporaneous with the ancient Sumerian and Egyptian civilizations, it was one of the most advanced civilizations of this time period.
     b. Its two major capitals were Mohenjo-daro and Harappa, which, like the other cities of the Indus civilization, featured a high citadel, lower domestic dwellings, an extensive sanitation system, and elaborate water baths.

---

[1]R. Pierce Beaver et al., eds., *Eerdmans' Handbook to the World's Religions* (Grand Rapids: Eerdmans, 1982), 170.

    c. Although archaeological digs have uncovered numerous tools, no weapons belonging to these people have been discovered. Thus some anthropologists argue that these people were pacifists.

    d. The abrupt decline of the Harappan civilization in the second millennium B.C. was quite possibly the result both of natural disasters and foreign invasions.

    e. To what extent Harappan religious thought contributed to the later emerging religions of India is uncertain, but evidently some elements have survived. Indeed, the phallic-shaped stones of this ancient society may have foreshadowed the linga (male sex organ) symbols of the Hindu god Siva (pronounced SHI-va).[2]

2. The earliest races to inhabit India were the Australoids and, more importantly, the Dravidians.

    a. In terms of agriculture, architecture, art, city planning, and dress, the Dravidians were culturally more advanced than the Aryans who conquered them.

    b. In fact, the Aryans adopted some of the Dravidian deities and religious ideas.

    c. "Hinduism," said Radhakrishnan, "has taken so much from the social life of the Dravadians, and other native, inhabitants."[3]

    d. Indeed, elements in Bhakti (devotion) Hinduism may have had their origin in Dravidian rituals.

C. The Vedic Period in India

1. The Aryans invaded India in the middle of the second millennium B.C. and, as the dominant race, developed their own culture and civilization in India.

    a. Evidently the nomadic Aryans had first settled in Persia (modern Iran) centuries earlier and then experienced a major split about 1500 B.C.

    b. Although some Aryan tribes migrated as far west as the Atlantic in Europe and as far east as Central Asia, most either remained in Persia and founded the Zoroastrian religion or relocated in India, where their religious views and practices assimilated with those of the indigenous Dravidians.

    c. The Aryan religion was expressed in hymns, which were later collected in sacred texts known as the Vedas.[4]

        (1) Vedic literature was composed during a thousand-year period beginning about 1400 B.C.

---

[2]The names and terms for which pronunciation is given in the text are not included in the glossary. See Part VI: Glossary for the pronunciation guide to many other terms.

[3]Sarvepalli Radhakrishnan, *Religion and Society* (London: Allen & Unwin, 1959), 101.

[4]See Part IV, Section I.A for a description of the Vedas.

(2) Vedic literature was passed down orally until written down centuries later, probably about the fourteenth century A.D.

d. The spoken language of the ancient Aryans was Sanskrit, which was also the language of the Vedas.

(1) The Sanskrit word *Veda* means "knowledge."

(2) The Brahmin priests taught that Sanskrit was the language of the gods and that the gods had conferred the Vedas to the ancient sages of India.

e. The early Vedic religion was primarily sacrificial in nature, emphasizing ritual offerings to numerous gods.

(1) The more important gods at this time were Varuna, believed to be the upholder of the moral and cosmic order;

(2) the warrior god Indra, to whom the largest number of hymns were dedicated in the Rg Veda;

(3) and the fire god Agni, who succeeded as the most influential god at this time because of his association with the fire sacrifice through which the people related to the gods.[5]

2. A class of Brahmin priests emerged by the first millennium B.C.

a. These priests established themselves as the highest caste in Indian society and not only dominated the religious life of the Indian people but also enacted social laws to govern the people.

b. This class of priests became known as "Brahmans"[6] because of their devotion to the god Brahman.

c. Over many centuries the popularity of certain gods, such as Brahma, Visnu, and Siva, became preeminent in the Indian pantheon and assumed the characteristics of lesser deities.[7]

D. Religious Unrest and Reform

1. The Aryans segregated Indian society into rigid classes.

a. This ancient Indian system of classification was known as *varna,* which means "color."

b. The Aryans themselves were divided into four groups: *Brahmins* (priests); *Ksatriyas* (warriors and rulers); *Vaisyas* (merchants); and *Sudra* (*Shudra*—laborers and servants); the "untouchables" (social outcastes today known as *Harijans*) were not included in this grouping since they were regarded as impure. Thus they were permitted little contact with the other classes.

---

[5]See Thomas J. Hopkins's excellent discussion of Agni's role in the religious life of the ancient people of India in *The Hindu Religious Tradition* (Belmont, Calif.: Wadsworth, 1971), 17–19.

[6]People use the term *Brahmin* to distinguish the word *Brahman* from its other meanings. See the glossary for the various definitions of *Brahman.*

[7]The term *henotheism* describes the phenomenon in which one god takes precedence in the worship of a people in a certain locality without denying the existence of other gods.

9

    c. Quite likely this grouping was originally an Aryan attempt to keep all other groups of people, particularly the indigenous inhabitants of India, separated from the Aryan nobility.

    d. The *Laws of Manu,* a legal and religious Hindu text, codified this system by the second century A.D.

    e. As time passed, this social system developed into what we know as the present caste system (*jati,* "birth groups"), which is now divided into numerous subcastes that are even more self-contained.

    f. The power structure of the Indian caste has changed dramatically.

      (1) Initially and until the modern era, the *varna* system was based on the religious belief that karma and samsara (the cycle of death and rebirth) dictated one's social station.

      (2) Hence, the spiritual leaders wielded the strongest powers in Indian society.

      (3) Today, however, since class distinctions are still in place and commerce and secular education have emerged in importance in contemporary Indian society, those groups with the most economic strength currently exert the most political influence.

2. Various religious movements arose in about the sixth century B.C. in protest against the spiritual tyranny of the Brahmin priesthood.

    a. Ancient Brahmanism had become spiritually sterile and morally corrupt in the hands of the priestly elite.

    b. Gifted thinkers such as Siddhartha Gautama (the *Buddha,* "the enlightened one") and Vardhamana Jnatrputra (*Mahavira,* "the great hero") rejected the Brahmin sacrificial system as a means to salvation (i.e., liberation from samsara). They denounced the religious dogma that supported the *varna* structure of society, which the Brahmin priests had insisted was divinely ordained.

    c. Thus new religions were born in India, including two of the best known still thriving today—Buddhism and Jainism.

3. Internal religious revival also occurred within ancient Brahmanism, which evolved into the religious orthodoxy of Hinduism.

    a. The sacred literature of the Hindus expanded to include not only the Vedas (*sruti;* see Part IV, Section I.A) but also other religious texts (*smrti;* see Part IV, Section I.B) that dramatically broadened the Indian religious philosophy and extended its ideas and practices beyond an elite few.

    b. The development of yoga systems shifted focus from the sacrificial ritual dominated by Brahmin priests to the teacher- (guru-) student relationship and the spiritual practices of the individual seeker.

      (1) Patanjali was the intellectual force behind the emergence of yoga as a major element in classical Hinduism.

      (2) He lived sometime in the fourth or fifth century A.D. and compiled earlier yoga traditions into the classic work *Yogasutra.*

    c. A third major element in the reformation of Hinduism was *bhakti*—devotion to a personal god, of which Siva and Krisna became two of the most popular.

E. Vedanta or Classical Hinduism

  1. During the first millennium A.D., six major schools of Hindu thought dominated the religious landscape of India.

    a. They included nyaya, vaisesika, samkhya, yoga, mimamsa, and vedanta.

    b. Each school subscribed to a particular *darsana,* that is, a way of looking at truth.

  2. Vedanta emerged as the predominant theological expression of Hindu philosophy.

    a. Vedanta means "end of the Veda," that is, the completion of all knowledge.

    b. Vedanta philosophy drew its ideas and inspiration primarily from the Upanisads, the mystical teachings that form the later Vedic writings.

    c. The most important system of Vedanta Hinduism is Advaita Vedanta, founded by Samkara (pronounced SHAN-ka-ra).

      (1) Samkara possibly was born in Kaladi in A.D 788 and passed away thirty-two years later.

      (2) Samkara taught that each person possesses an individual soul (Atman) that is related to the Universal Soul (Brahman), which is unique and nondualistic.

      (3) Samkara also said that all distinctions are unreal. In other words, since all reality is one, whatever distinctions we perceive are mental illusions.

      (4) Samkara's darsana became the cornerstone to the monistic philosophy of classical Hinduism.

II. Historical Background (Contemporary)

A. Contemporary Hinduism

  1. The path of devotion (*bhakti*) best describes the religious life of most Hindus in India for the past millennium.

    a. Most of these people worship either Siva (Saivism) or an avatar (i.e., an incarnation) of Visnu (Vaisnavism).

    b. The Bhagavad-Gita and the Puranas are the scriptural texts that have provided these people with their understanding of these gods.

    c. P. H. Ashby says, "Moksa [personal salvation from the cycle of rebirth] is available to men and women as a result of the gracious love bestowed by the Adorable One to those who adore God in whatever form is most meaningful to them."[8]

2. During this time dynamic holy men inspired the masses with their messages.

   a. Ramananda (1400–1470) urged people to worship Rama, an avatar of Visnu.

      (1) Instead of teaching in Sanskrit as other Hindu scholars had done, he preached in their daily language.

      (2) He challenged caste distinctions among believers.

      (3) He taught that Visnu loved humanity and sought to save it from evil through his human incarnation, Rama.

   b. Caitanya (pronounced chi-TAN-ya; 1486–1533) espoused a passionate devotion to Krisna, another avatar of Visnu.

      (1) He also preached to all the castes.

      (2) He declared Krisna the total embodiment of the divine, thus not only exalting Krisna above all deities but also incorporating the divine qualities of all the other gods into Krisna.

   c. Ram Mohan Roy (1772–1833) was one of the leading voices of the Reform Movements in India in the early nineteenth century.

      (1) He was a Brahmin intellectual who had been educated in Sanskrit, English, and Persian.

      (2) Although he was a monotheist and admirer of Jesus, he rejected Jesus' divinity.

   d. Ramakrishna (1836–1886) spearheaded the Hindu Renaissance in the nineteenth century.

      (1) Hindus regard him as both a spiritual genius and an enlightened saint.

      (2) C. S. J. White said, "People began to call him *Paramahamsa,* 'The Supreme Swan,' the title of greatest dignity in the Hindu ascetic tradition."[9]

      (3) After experimenting with Vedanta, Hindu monotheism, tantra, Islam, and Christianity, he taught that all religions provide different paths to the same god.

      (4) His disciples established the Ramakrishna Mission, which has become a worldwide organization whose purpose is to spread his teachings globally.

   e. Aurobindo Ghose (1872–1950) was a celebrated writer who appealed to Hindu intellectuals for his defense of Indian culture and Hindu philosophy.

---

[8]P. H. Ashby, "Hinduism," in *The Perennial Dictionary of World Religions,* ed. Keith Crum (San Francisco: Harper Collins, 1989), 314.

[9]C. S. J. White, "Ramakrishna," in *The Perennial Dictionary of World Religions,* 598.

(1) During his studies in England at Cambridge, he won several prestigious awards for his academic work.

(2) Hindus highly revere Aurobindo as an outstanding poet and charismatic spiritual leader who espoused a life devoted to meditation.

f. Sarvepalli Radhakrishnan (1888–1975) was one of the most important Hindu philosophers to spread the teachings of Hinduism to the West.

(1) Radhakrishnan was also an eminent scholar who taught at Oxford in England and an accomplished statesman who was president of India (1962–1967).

(2) Although he encouraged harmony among all religions, he advocated the spiritual superiority of Advaita Vedanta.

B. Hinduism in North America

1. The Transcendentalist Movement of the Mid-nineteenth Century

   a. Since the arrival of the pilgrims in New England in the seventeenth century, religious freedom has been a cornerstone of American society.

   b. "In the past four centuries many people with differing spiritual beliefs have left their footprints on American shores. It is not surprising, therefore, that Eastern mystical leaders have traveled here to leave their impressions in the sand. What *is* surprising is that so many people, particularly Christians, are startled to learn that this is occurring and regard it as a contemporary phenomenon. One only needs to read the works of Emerson and Thoreau to realize that Eastern mysticism took root in America long before the twentieth century."[10]

   c. Ralph Waldo Emerson (1803–1882) advanced his doctrine of the "Oversoul," which expressed a pantheistic worldview and was a result of his understanding of Brahman and karma, in his philosophy and poetry.

   d. The Upanisads and Bhagavad-Gita inspired Henry David Thoreau (1817–1862) when he wrote *Walden* and other influential works.

   e. The Transcendentalists, in turn, have had profound influence on both Western and Eastern thinkers (such as Mohandas Gandhi [1869–1948]).

2. Swami Vivekananda (1863–1902) and the American Vedanta Societies

   a. After the death of his master, Sri Ramakrishna, Vivekananda traveled throughout the world, spreading the teachings of his departed master and participating in the founding of the Ramakrishna Mission.

---

[10]Jerry Yamamoto, "Footprints in the Sand," *Spiritual Counterfeits Project Newsletter* (October-November 1978): 1.

    b. He spoke against the Indian caste system, championed the rights of women and the poor, and commended Western science and technology while preaching the Vedanta philosophy.

    c. In 1893 he attended the World Parliament of Religions in Chicago, where he instantly attracted a wide following of North Americans, who were fascinated with his charismatic persona in his striking red robes and his articulate English-spoken lectures that "stressed the principles of the Vedanta philosophy with humanitarian service."[11]

    d. In 1897 Vivekananda's American followers established American Vedanta Societies, first in New York and Boston, and then throughout North America.

    e. While still being spiritually linked to the Ramakrishna Mission, the American Vedanta Societies have influenced such Western intellectuals as Aldous Huxley, Gertrude Stein, Christopher Isherwood, and William James.

3. A New Wave of Gurus and Swamis

    a. Paramahansa Yogananda (1893–1952) was one of the first Indian missionaries to settle in the United States and has had remarkable influence over countless Americans seeking Eastern mystical experiences with his published memoirs, *Autobiography of a Yogi.*

    b. In 1976 the Himalayan Institute sponsored the first International Yoga and Meditation Conference in Chicago where many Westerners were able to listen to the messages of Swami Rama, Swami Satchidananda, and other spiritual leaders of mission-minded Hindu orders for the first time.[12]

    c. Other influential Indian spiritual masters who have created a notable following in the West are Satya Sai Baba (India's internationally famous faith healer who heads the Spiritual Advancement of the Individual Foundation; b. 1926), Sri Chinmoy (a popular lecturer and writer, who teaches various techniques of yoga; b. 1931), Swami Muktananda (a popular teacher of Siddha Yoga; 1908–1982), and Bhagwan Rajneesh (a controversial guru who espouses a hodge-podge of Eastern ideas; b. 1931).

    d. Despite the tremendous success many of these swamis and gurus have had in North America, "only certain aspects of Hinduism have been appropriated by Americans," said Juergensmeyer. "Philosophic and mystical teachings and the fellowship of religious movements have had wider appeal in America than Hindu con-

---

[11]Jerry Yamamoto, "Swami Vivekananda," *Spiritual Counterfeits Project Newsletter* (April-May 1979): 1.

[12]I attended this conference and personally interviewed several of these charismatic religious leaders, such as Swami Satchidananda (a disciple of Swami Sivananda, a celebrated guru in India), who have become widely popular among Western dabblers into Eastern mysticism.

cepts of ritual and familial duties or Hindu customary practices and divine mythologies."[13]

e. The two most notable expressions of the appeal of Hinduism in North America in the past thirty years have been Transcendental Meditation and the Hare Krishna movement.

C. Maharishi Mahesh Yogi and Transcendental Meditation (TM)

1. Maharishi's Success in the West

   a. Born in 1911, Maharishi earned a B.S. degree in physics from the University of Allahabad in India in 1941 and then became a disciple of Swami Brahmananda Saraswati ("Guru Dev," or "Divine Teacher"), one of the most popular gurus in India after World War II.

      (1) *Maharishi* means "great seer" or "great sage," a title he assumed after attaining a specific level of spirituality in Hinduism.

      (2) *Mahesh* is his family name; he was born Mahesh Prasad Varma.

      (3) *Yogi* means "master of yoga."

   b. At the monastery of Jyotir Math, Maharishi was trained in yoga and the teachings of Samkara, who had asserted the Hindu philosophy of monism (i.e., the unity and oneness of all creation).

      (1) Maharishi would later modify his master's teachings into a simplified form for Westerners.

      (2) The TM organization purports that Maharishi's philosophy reflects an Indian tradition that is thousands of years old.

   c. After the death of his master in 1953, Maharishi secluded himself in a Himalayan cave in "the Valley of the Saints" for two years before he gathered his own following in Southern India.

      (1) Although Maharishi has maintained his original center in Rishikesh, India, he has never had a wide appeal in India.

      (2) Later he would establish his international headquarters in Switzerland.

      (3) He would also move Maharishi International University to Fairfield, Iowa, in 1974.

   d. In 1959 he made his first attempt to capture American interest when he came to the United States to impart his simplified style of meditation.

      (1) His initial excursions into the West were considerably less successful than he had hoped, largely because he did little to disguise the religious content of his teachings.

      (2) His international popularity temporarily surged in the mid-1960s when he initiated the Beatles and the Beach Boys into

---

[13]M. Juergensmeyer, "Hinduism in America," in *The Perennial Dictionary of World Religions*, 318.

the practice of his method of yogic meditation, called "Transcendental Meditation" (TM).

(3) After a stunning setback in public interest in TM in the late sixties, Maharishi scored a remarkable comeback. "In its heyday in the midseventies," observes researcher David Haddon, "TM was called the McDonald's of meditation because of its extravagantly successful packaging of Eastern meditation for the American mass market."[14]

(4) Maharishi had assigned talented Americans with marketing expertise[15] to present TM as a scientifically proven method of achieving relaxation and inner peace. This marketing effort proved to be immensely successful.

(a) Westerners wanted to give little commitment while receiving instant results, which the TM organization offered.

(b) In addition, TM instructors assured Westerners that TM was a technique that could be practiced without violating one's own religious beliefs. Indeed, TM would help one become a better Christian, Hindu, or simply a better person (if one was an atheist).

(c) Thus the religious roots of TM were disregarded while being touted as a scientific panacea. The practice of TM was called "the Science of Creative Intelligence," while religious references to TM were avoided.

(d) "TM became the quintessential self-help technique for dealing with the stresses of modern life."[16]

2. TM's Eventual Decline and Altered Public Image

a. The TM movement in North America reached its peak in the mid-1970s and then declined after that, for several reasons.

(1) It could not deliver on all the benefits the TM organization promised to initiated meditators.

(2) Eastern philosophy had saturated North American society to the extent that religious seekers wanted more powerful spiritual experiences, which other Far Eastern groups offered while not disguising their religious nature.

(3) Since TM did not demand staunch commitment from its practitioners, only a small percentage have become lifelong devotees of the Maharishi.

---

[14]David Haddon, "Transcendental Meditation," in *A Guide to Cults and New Religions,* ed. Ronald Enroth et al. (Downers Grove, Ill.: InterVarsity Press, 1983), 136.

[15]One such person was Jerry Jarvis, who became national director of Maharishi's first significant organization in the United States, the Students' International Meditation Society (SIMS).

[16]Marcia Greene, "From Religion to Science to Siddhis: The Evolution of the TM Movement," *Spiritual Counterfeits Project Journal* (Winter 1984): 57.

(4) Several legal rulings in the United States established TM courses as religious in nature, which severely hampered its efforts to enter schools and receive federal and state aid.[17]

b. In 1977 the TM organization tried to recover its international sparkle by launching its Sidhi program.

(1) TM representatives claimed that meditators can learn to levitate (or "fly") and become invisible in this program.

(2) According to Hindu teachings, those yogins who attain higher stages of yoga through mastery of yogic practices acquire paranormal psychic powers, known as *siddhis,*[18] which literally means "accomplishment."

(3) Despite the disappointing response of Americans to TM's Sidhi program, Maharishi and TM "likely [have] had a direct influence on more Americans than any other single Hindu movement or teacher."[19]

D. Prabhupada and the Hare Krishna Movement

1. Origins

a. The three most important deities in the Hindu pantheon are Brahma (creator), Siva (destroyer), and Visnu (preserver), known as the *trimurti.*

b. Visnu is preeminent among all the gods to the Vaisnavites (worshipers of Visnu), who consider him "the primal person and the first-born of creation, who has neither beginning nor end. In fact, Visnu appears to be regarded by his devotees as the sole source of the universe, active in all three of its phases: creation, preservation and dissolution."[20]

c. Visnu's most important feature is as preserver and protector of the universe, which he accomplishes through his many incarnations, known as avatars.

(1) The ten most famous avatars of Visnu include Matsya, the Fish; Kurma, the Tortoise; Varaha, the Boar; Vamana, the Dwarf; Narasimha, the Man-Lion; Parasurama, Rama, Krisna, and Buddha,[21] men with various attributes; and Kalkin, the avatar to come.

---

[17]In the case of *Malnak* v. *Maharishi Mahesh Yogi* in 1977, Judge H. Curtis Meanor of the U.S. District Court at Newark, N.J., ruled that TM is religious and could not be taught in the public school system. In 1979, TM lost its appeal in the U.S. Court of Appeals for the Third Circuit in Philadelphia, Pa.

[18]The Sanskrit word is *siddhi,* whereas in the TM movement it is spelled with one "d" for trademark purposes.

[19]Juergensmeyer, "Transcendental Meditation," in *The Perennial Dictionary of World Religions,* 765.

[20]Cornelia Dimmitt and J. A. van Buitenen, *Classical Hindu Mythology: A Reader in the Sanskrit Puranas* (Philadelphia: Temple University Press, 1978), 59.

[21]In reaction to the early Buddhist movement in India, the Hindus sought to diminish the Buddha's impact by including him as an avatar of Visnu, but asserting that the Buddha came to deceive those who were unfit to be true adherents of the Vedic tradition.

      (2) Krisna, the eighth avatar, is the best loved among the majority of the followers of Visnu.

      (3) In fact, worship of Krisna has superseded the adoration of Visnu among many Vaisnavites.

    d. Caitanya Mahaprabhu, a Bengalese Brahmin, founded the Krisnaite sect in the sixteenth century.

      (1) He taught that the best way to burn off ignorance and karma (the consequences of previous bad actions) and achieve perfect bliss is to express loving devotion (*bhakti*) through dancing and chanting to Krisna.

      (2) Although traditional Hindus frowned on his unorthodox, public display of worship of Krisna, Caitanya attracted a wide and devoted following because of his argumentative brilliance and personal charisma.

2. Prabhupada's Success in the West

    a. Although most Indians view the Hare Krishna movement with amusement and as an American phenomenon, this group cannot be divorced from its Hindu roots in India.

    b. Abhay Charan De Bhaktivedanta Swami Prabhupada (1896–1977) founded this organization, whose formal name is the International Society for Krishna Consciousness (ISKCON) in India.

      (1) Prabhupada, who was born Abhay Charan, was a successful pharmaceutical businessman in Bengal before he renounced his secular life and commenced a lifelong devotion to the teachings of Caitanya and worship of Krisna.

      (2) In 1944 he conveyed his religious views in English in a magazine entitled *Back to Godhead*. At this time he was referred to as "Bhaktivedanta," which means "devotional knowledge."

      (3) In 1965 he came to New York City and established temples throughout the United States. Three years later his young American disciples honored him with the name "Prabhupada," which means "at whose feet masters sit."

    c. Before his death, Prabhupada personally selected twenty-four senior devotees to serve on the Governing Body Commission, which directs the operations and missionary work of the organization.

      (1) Instead of picking a successor, as is customary in Hindu tradition, Prabhupada left his movement in the hands of several disciples.

      (2) Following Prabhupada's death in 1977 in India, members of ISKCON have continued to spread the teachings of their master throughout the world.

      (3) "The Hare Krishna movement has become established in India at the Krishna pilgrimage center, Vrindavan, where

American devotees attempt to convert Indians to the movement."[22]

d. Most members of ISKCON are Westerners, who have adopted Indian names and donned saffron garments, with the men shaving their heads in the tradition of Indian holy men.

e. Their temples are replicas of those constructed in India, and in them they worship the image of deities.

E. Asian Indians in the United States

1. Immigration Figures

   a. Only 1,957 Asian Indians resided in the United States between 1899 and 1907.

   b. Increasing numbers of Asian Indians migrated to the United States during the early twentieth century, but they encountered racial persecutions as Asians, being identified with Chinese and Japanese immigrants.

      (1) In 1923 the U.S. Supreme Court ruled that "Hindus" were ineligible for U.S. citizenship.

      (2) In 1946, however, Asian Indians were allowed to come to the United States and seek citizenship.

      (3) In the following year, India became an independent nation, and Asian Indians were encouraged to emigrate to the United States.

   c. After passing the Immigration and Nationality Act of 1965, the U.S. government eliminated national quotas, and Asian-Indian immigration soared.

      (1) It is estimated that 387,000 Asian Indians lived in the United States by 1980.

      (2) "By 1989, estimates of Asian Indians in the United States approached 700,000; by the year 2000, this number will be close to a million."[23]

2. Sociological Profile

   a. The largest concentrations of Asian Indians are in the metropolitan areas of major cities in the United States.

      (1) The New York metropolitan area, the greater Los Angeles metropolitan area, and the San Francisco Bay area support the highest numbers.

      (2) Several thousand Asian Indians also dwell in and around the big cities in Illinois, Maryland, Massachusetts, Michigan, Ohio, Oregon, Pennsylvania, Texas, and Washington.

---

[22]Juergensmeyer, "Hinduism in America," in *The Perennial Dictionary of World Religions*, 321.

[23]Richard A. K. Shankar, "Asian Indian Americans," in *Encyclopedia of Multiculturalism*, ed. Susan Auerbach (New York: Marshall Cavendish, 1994), 1:214.

b. Asian Indians use English as their primary mode of communication.

(1) A wide diversity of Indian languages is spoken within their ethnic groups.

(2) Since they are able to speak English fluently, their transition into the mainstream of American life in the past three decades has been relatively smooth.

III. Vital Statistics

A. *Population Figures*[24]

1. India

a. 700 million Hindus reside in India.

b. They comprise 82 percent of India's population.

2. Major Presence of Hinduism in Other Countries

a. 11 percent in Bangladesh

b. 25 percent in Bhutan

c. 41 percent in Fiji

d. 50 percent in Mauritius

e. 89 percent in Nepal (the only nation where Hinduism is the state religion)

f. 15 percent in Sri Lanka

g. 27 percent in Surinam

h. 25 percent in Trinidad

3. Additional Figures

a. More than one million Hindus live in North America.

b. More than two million Hindus live on the Indonesian island of Bali.

c. About 13 percent of the world's population are Hindus.

B. *Selected Literature*

1. *Ananda Marga Review.* Corona, N.Y.: Ananda Marga (quarterly)

2. *Beads of Truth.* Los Angeles: 3HO Foundation (quarterly)

3. *Collaboration.* Berkeley, Calif.: Sri Aurobindo Association (quarterly)

4. *Hinduism Today.* Kapaa, Hawaii: Himalayan Academy (monthly)

5. *International Yoga Guide.* Miami: Yoga Research Foundation (monthly)

6. *Satyavani.* Greenbelt, Md.: Friends of India Society International (monthly)

---

[24]Dean C. Halverson, ed., *The Compact Guide to World Religions* (Minneapolis: Bethany House, 1996), 87.

7. *Self-Realization Magazine.* Los Angeles: Self-Realization Fellowship (quarterly)

8. *Yoga International.* Honesdale, Pa.: Himalayan International Institute (bimonthly)

9. *Yoga Journal.* Berkeley, Calif.: California Yoga Teachers Association (bimonthly)

C. *Major Asian-Indian and Hindu Organizations*

1. Ananda Marga Yoga Society, with headquarters in Corona, N.Y., promotes Karma Yoga and meditation practices.

2. Association of Asian Indians in America with headquarters in Muttontown, N.Y., promotes Indian cultural activities in the United States.

3. Friends of India Society International, with headquarters in Greenbelt, Md., seeks to improve the image of Indian culture in North America.

4. Integral Yoga Institute, in Buckingham, Va., instructs on the teachings of Swami Satchidanada and Hatha Yoga.

5. International Society for Krishna Consciousness (ISKCON), in New York, promotes the teachings of Prabhupada and devotion to Krisna.

6. Maharishi Vedic University, which is program-based with no national headquarters, conducts initiations into Transcendental Meditation and courses on the teachings of Maharishi Mahesh Yogi.

7. Ramakrishna-Vivekananda Center (and Vedanta Societies), in New York, is a missionary outreach center of the Ramakrishna Order of India that teaches Vedanta philosophy to Westerners.

8. Self-Realization Fellowship, with headquarters in Los Angeles, promotes the teachings of Paramahansa Yogananda and the scientific practice of yoga.

9. Spiritual Advancement of the Individual Foundation, with a national center in Oakland, Calif., promotes the teachings of Satya Sai Baba and Siddha Yoga.

10. Sri Aurobindo Association, with headquarters in Berkeley, Calif., spreads the teachings of Aurobindo.

11. 3HO/Sikh Dharma Brotherhood (formerly the Happy/Healthy/Holy Organization), with headquarters in Los Angeles, spreads the teachings of Yogi Bhajan and Kundalini and Hatha Yoga (though emphasis has now shifted to the Sikh tradition).[25]

12. Yoga Research Foundation, with headquarters in Miami teaches Vedanta philosophy and Integral Yoga, which combines the major methods of yoga.

---

[25]The Sikh religion was primarily formed by Guru Nanak (1469–1539) in India, drawing from the teachings of Bhakti Hinduism and Muslim Sufis.

21

Part II: Theology

I. Hindu View of History

A. The Hindu Position on History Briefly Stated

1. The history of the world is eternally cyclical.
2. The gods revere a great serpent (Sesa), who sustains the world.
3. In the last of the four major ages (Kali Age), all of humanity will be completely destroyed.

B. Arguments Used by Hindus to Support Their Position on History

1. The history of the world is eternally cyclical.

   a. Hindus measure time in accordance with the life of their creator god, Brahma.

      (1) The lifetime of Brahma is 12,000 divine years, with 360 human years being the length of one divine year.[1]

      (2) According to Dimmitt and van Buitenen, "The universe endures as long as the god lives, then dies as he dies; a periodic dissolution of all forms coincides with the ending of Brahma's life."[2]

      (3) Brahma is then born again from a cosmic egg and the cycle repeats and continues to repeat endlessly.

   b. The Puranas, Hindu sacred texts, divide time into four recurring ages (or *yugas*).[3]

      (1) "In the first Age, the Krta, there was virtue; it continued throughout the Treta; becoming confused in the Dvapara, it is lost altogether in the Kali."[4]

      (2) The length of each age is, for the Krta Yuga, 4,800 divine years; the Treta Yuga, 3,600 divine years; the Dvapara Yuga, 2,400 divine years; the Kali Yuga, 1,200 divine years.

   c. "The four Ages as a unit are understood to repeat in a continual and endless cycle."[5]

      (1) Each age progressively decreases in length just as the world and humanity become increasingly evil and morally corrupt.

---

[1] The Puranas depict a single lifetime of Brahma to be 4,320,000 human years.

[2] Cornelia Dimmitt and J. A. van Buitenen, *Classical Hindu Mythology: A Reader in the Sanskrit Puranas* (Philadelphia: Temple University Press, 1978), 19.

[3] See Markandeya Purana (43.3–44) and Kurma Purana (1.27.16–57).

[4] Kurma Purana 1.27.57.

[5] Dimmitt and van Buitenen, *Classical Hindu Mythology*, 21.

(2) Hindu doctrine teaches that we are currently living in the Kali Age when humanity is at its worst.

2. The gods revere a great serpent (Sesa), who sustains the world.

  a. Sesa (pronounced SHA-shu) is lord of the snakes.

    (1) Although the worship of snakes is ancient in India, Sesa does not appear until the writing of the Mahabharata (c. 400 B.C.).

    (2) In Indian art Sesa is depicted as the thousand-headed serpent.

  b. Sesa means "remainder" in Sanskrit.

    (1) Hindu texts say that Sesa destroyed all the worlds at the end of the Kali Yuga with fire from his mouth.

    (2) After this cataclysmic destruction of the worlds, Sesa was created from the residue that was left—hence the meaning of his name.

    (3) He is also called Ananta, which means "endless."

  c. Sesa is associated with the three major Hindu gods.

    (1) According to Hindu myths, Sesa pleased the creator god Brahma with his piety, and thus Brahma accorded him the honor of bearing the earth.[6]

      (a) While Sesa's serpentine coils encircle the earth, he carries the earth on his head.

      (b) Thus Sesa is regarded as the foundation of the earth.

    (2) Sesa is also said to be born of the destroyer god Siva, becoming the axle of his divine vehicle.

    (3) Sesa, however, is mostly linked with the sustainer god Visnu, who is often portrayed reclining on Sesa.

  d. In fact, Sesa is "revered by all the gods,"[7] having the characteristics of righteousness, peace, and asceticism.

3. In the last of the four major ages (Kali Age), all of humanity will be completely destroyed.

  a. By the end of each Kali Yuga, humanity degenerates to the depth of evil.

    (1) The current Kali Age began at the end of the Mahabharata war toward the close of the fourth millenium B.C.,[8] and it will last for more than 400,000 years longer from this present time.

    (2) Human greed is the root of human suffering, and this greed increasingly prevails in the Kali Age.

    (3) In addition, selfishness is the source of war, disease, and death.

---

[6]Mahabharata Adiparvan 12.356–64.
[7]Visnu Purana 4.1–10.
[8]Hindus believe the Mahabharata war is historical, while many historians think it is myth.

(4) Other characteristics of the Kali Age are that people will forget the Vedas; different social classes will mix with one another; and deceit, murder, and famine will become more common.

(5) Hindus divide sins into three major categories, all of which become more prevalent in the Kali Age.

   (a) Violating social customs, such as dishonoring one's family and showing no respect to Brahmin priests.

   (b) Not maintaining purity of body, such as eating cow meat.

   (c) Committing evil behavior, such as stealing and killing.

b. Decay of the world and humanity is a natural process, whose inevitable result is the destruction of creation.[9]

(1) After the earth becomes bare of vegetation because of increasing human perversions, all living beings physically die of starvation.

(2) The sun then scorches the earth, drying it of all water.

(3) The world is enflamed until a cosmic rain douses the fire and floods the entire earth.

(4) As a result, nothing exists except for this cosmic ocean, which has absorbed the spiritual remains of created beings, who anticipate being reborn in the next creation.

(5) Brahma's life comes to an end at the conclusion of the Kali Age, and then he is born again from this cosmic ocean, at which time Brahma creates the universe again.

C. *Refutation of Arguments Used by Hindus to Support Their Position on History*

1. The Hindu concept of time is without scientific support and conflicts with historical scholarship.

a. There is no evidence that the present creation has a life span of 4,320,000 years, as asserted by the Hindu sacred texts (Puranas).

(1) Science can only guess as to the age of the universe. Therefore, science can neither confirm nor refute this Hindu figure.

(2) No sacred literature independent of Hindu scriptures concurs with this assertion.

b. The Hindu classification and description of the four ages is flawed in light of what is known of the ancient history of India.

(1) According to the Puranas, the Vedas existed from the beginning of creation,[10] and in the Kali Age, which began about five thousand years ago, people "are ignorant of the Vedas" and "recite the Vedas incorrectly."[11]

---

[9]See Visnu Parana 6.3.14–41; 4.1–10 for this account of final dissolution.
[10]Matsya Purana 3.1-12.
[11]Kurma Purana 1.28.1-7.

(2) Yet historians contend that the Aryans did not migrate into India before the third millennium B.C., and the Vedas emerged thereafter.

(3) In the "General Introduction" to *A Sourcebook in Indian Philosophy,* which provides the texts and commentary to key Hindu scriptures, Hindu scholar Sarvepalli Radhakrishnan and Charles Moore stated, "The Vedic Period is dimmed by obscurity, but it may be placed approximately between 2500 and 600 B.C. This is the period during which the Aryans, having come down into India from central Asia, settled their new homeland and gradually expanded and developed their Aryan culture and civilization.... The literature of this period consists of the four Vedas (*Rg Veda, Yajur Veda, Sama Veda,* and *Atharva Veda*).... The Mantras [from these Vedas] ... constitute the actual beginning of Indian philosophy."[12]

c. The cyclical view of time is untenable and leads to human despair.

(1) The transition from one creation cycle to the next is illogical since each cycle corresponds to the life cycle of the creator god Brahma.

(a) If the life of the creator ends with the dissolution of his creation, then a greater force must have caused the rebirth of Brahma to create again.

(b) And if that force can mastermind the same sequence of ages (the four *yugas*) within every cycle, as opposed to being subject to random chance, then this force must be intelligent.

(c) Yet Hindu philosophy cannot logically explain what this intelligent force is and why it has designed something that goes forever in a circle but has no ultimate goal.

(2) Also, believing that all things must continuously repeat this cycle inspires little, if any, hope for eternal joy and peace.

(a) Even if we achieve union with Brahman and bliss-consciousness with Krisna, we must be created again in the next cycle and go through the same sequences of sin, suffering, death, rebirth, spiritual discipline, and self-realization.

(b) If all things are absorbed in Brahman at the end of each cycle anyway, the desire for liberation from ignorance and the effort to achieve self-illumination diminishes further for most people.

---

[12]Sarvepalli Radhakrishnan and Charles A. Moore, eds., *A Sourcebook in Indian Philosophy* (Princeton, N.J.: Princeton University Press, 1957), xvii–xviii.

2. The religious significance of Sesa is dubious and ominous.
   a. The Puranas' account of Sesa's destruction-creation roles[13] is illogical.
      (1) On the one hand, the Puranas say that Sesa destroyed the worlds.
      (2) On the other hand, the Puranas say that Sesa was created from the "remains" of the worlds he destroyed.
      (3) It is argued that Sesa emerges from the residue of one cycle and then becomes the destroyer of the worlds in the next cycle.
      (4) The problem, however, is that then countless preexistent Sesas exist at the time of each of his creations, which is confounding unless Sesa also destroys himself at the time of dissolution.
      (5) The Hindu scriptures do not indicate that this occurred; in fact, the differing accounts of Sesa at the end and beginning of cycles make this possibility extremely ambiguous.
   b. The reverence given to the serpent is an affront to God and demeaning to humanity.

      (1) Even within Hindu scriptures, Sesa the serpent is depicted as a created being.
      (2) Moreover, when the Hindus worship snakes, they are worshiping actual creatures.
      (3) That gods worship a created being is the same as saying the Creator worships the beast of the field.
      (4) In his explanation of Romans 1:25, biblical scholar James D. G. Dunn comments on this misdirected homage this way: "Paul points again to the root cause of humankind's corrupted and dishonoring state. They exchanged what they knew to be the truth of God for a lie; they preferred to direct their devotion to the creature instead of the Creator. Here the echo of Gen 3 is even stronger. Adam/man believed the serpent's calumny and deception ('You will not die . . .; you will be like God' [Gen 3:4–5]). And the result? Not that he became independent and god-like, but rather that he became caught in a baser dependence, a dependence on things; he became less than human, the creature of creatures rather than of the Creator. As Paul himself implies so clearly, man the creature is bound by his very nature to worship and serve something beyond himself. So that if he rejects the only one worthy of his worship and service, it is inevitable that he will direct that basic drive toward an inferior object and thus reduce his own stature in consequence. Who would think to choose as one's master the created thing

---

[13]See R. N. Minor, "Sesa, Shesa," in *The Perennial Dictionary of World Religions*, ed. Keith Crum (San Francisco: Harper Collins, 1989), 672.

rather than the glorious Creator? But that is just what man has done."[14]

(5) The worship of the creature is folly to those who know the Creator.

3. The Hindu teaching on human evil and universal desolation is self-defeating.

a. Although Hindu texts indicate that we are living in the last age when humanity has sunk to the depth of moral corruption, even revered Hindu teachers cannot proclaim such an unpleasant message to the world.

(1) In fact, many gurus and swamis have come to the West, promoting harmony among all peoples by extolling the goodness of humanity.

(2) For instance, Swami Vivekananda, founder of the Vedanta societies, declared at the first World Parliament of Religions in Chicago in 1893, "It's a sin to call a man a sinner."

(3) Although Judeo-Christian doctrine teaches that all humanity is fallen and sinful, it also asserts that people can be delivered from this condition without their personal identity being lost in a cosmic ocean.

b. Although Hindu scriptures predict that all humankind will be destroyed, Hindu leaders cannot admit to the hopelessness of this kind of fate for humanity.

(1) Spiritual Hindu leaders have promised that worldwide compliance to their teachings will lead to a golden age for the human race.

(2) For example, Maharishi Mahesh Yogi called this wonderful time the "Age of Enlightenment," as described in his book *Transcendental Meditation.*[15]

(3) Moreover, Maharishi founded the Spiritual Regeneration Movement in the late 1950s "with the sole purpose of spiritually regenerating the lives of all men in every part of the world"[16] in order to usher in this "Age of Enlightenment."

(4) Despite the efforts of all dedicated Hindus to create a time of universal peace and goodwill, they cannot dismiss their own scriptures that predict the total annihilation of the human race at the end of this Kali Yuga.

---

[14]James D. G. Dunn, *Romans 1—8,* in *Word Biblical Commentary* (Dallas: Word, 1988), 73.

[15]Maharishi Mahesh Yogi, *Transcendental Meditation* (New York: Signet Books, 1968). The original title of this book was *The Science of Being and Art of Living.*

[16]Maharishi Mahesh Yogi, *Maharishi Mahesh Yogi on the Bhagavad-Gita* (Baltimore: Penguin Books, 1969), 21.

(5) Christian doctrine also warns of a desolation to come, but those who follow Christ will be spared from eternal damnation and commune with the Lord Jesus forever, which gives believers an assured hope for future happiness.

D. *Arguments Used to Prove the Biblical Doctrine on History to Hindus*

1. God is independent of time, which is not cyclical but linear.

   a. God is not bound to any life cycle.

      (1) Jesus said he and his heavenly Father existed before the creation of the world, for he prayed, "And now, Father, glorify me in your presence with the glory I had with you before the world began" (John 17:5).

      (2) Moreover, God the Father and his Son have always enjoyed a personal, loving relationship, as indicated in Jesus' words to God, "You loved me before the creation of the world" (v. 24).

      (3) Unlike Brahma, who is subject to the endless cycles of death and rebirth according to Hindu sacred writings, God has always existed, being transcendent from his creation and personal in his character.

   b. Although the Bible does not divide human history into distinct ages, it does mark the earthly ministry of Jesus and the second coming of Christ as *the* crucial events that radically alter human history.

      (1) From Creation to Jesus' earthly birth, God had arranged for Jesus' public ministry.

         (a) Jesus said, "Everything must be fulfilled that is written about me in the Law of Moses, the Prophets and the Psalms" (Luke 24:44).

         (b) God's "mystery" [i.e., God's plan for humanity and purpose in Christ] had "been kept hidden for ages and generations, but is now disclosed to the saints" (Col. 1:26), meaning after Jesus completed his earthly ministry.

      (2) In the future, when Christ returns to earth, the last judgment will occur and the Lord's faithful followers will join him in everlasting and heavenly glory.

         (a) The apostle Paul assured Christians of this great hope when he wrote to the Thessalonian believers, "For the Lord himself will come down from heaven, . . . and the dead in Christ will rise first. After that, we who are still alive and are left will be caught up together with them in the clouds to meet the Lord in the air. And so we will be with the Lord forever" (1 Thess. 4:16–17).

         (b) The apostle Peter said, "The present heavens and earth are reserved for fire, being kept for the day of judgment and destruction of ungodly men" (2 Peter 3:7; see also Jude 14–15).

(c) To Christ's faithful, the Lord will say from his throne in heavenly glory, "Come, you who are blessed by my Father; take your inheritance, the kingdom prepared for you since the creation of the world" (Matt. 25:34).

(d) Thus the unrighteous "will go away to eternal punishment, but the righteous to eternal life" (v. 46).

c. Christ will reign over his kingdom forever (Rev. 11:15).

(1) Thus there is no end to God and his omnipotence (see Dan. 7:27; 1 Cor. 4:20; Jude 25).

(2) Indeed, "Jesus Christ is the same yesterday and today and forever" (Heb. 13:8).

(3) Therefore time is not cyclical but subject to the will of Jesus Christ, who has supreme authority over "all things" (Eph. 1:20–22).

2. Scripture portrays the "ancient serpent" as utterly evil and the defeated enemy of God.

a. God condemns the worship of all created beings, including the serpent.

(1) The Lord God *made* the serpent that beguiled the first man and the first woman (Gen. 2:17).

(2) Therefore "the wrath of God is being revealed from heaven against all the godliness and wickedness of men who suppress the truth by their wickedness, . . . They exchanged the truth of God for a lie, and worshiped and served created things rather than the Creator. . . . Now we know that God's judgment against those who do such things is based on truth" (Rom. 1:18, 25; 2:2).

b. The "ancient serpent" is Satan, the devil (Rev. 12:9; 20:2).

(1) The serpent was "crafty" (Gen. 3:1) and "cunning" in tempting the first man and the first woman to disobey God, which led to the fall of humanity (2 Cor. 11:3).

(2) The "ancient serpent," Satan, not only deceives the world (Rev. 12:9), but also entered Judas Iscariot and persuaded him to betray Jesus (Luke 22:3).

(3) Satan also takes God's Word away from people (Mark 4:15) and "masquerades as an angel of light" (2 Cor. 11:14).

c. God vanquishes Satan.

(1) After the serpent beguiled Adam and Eve, God cursed the serpent, telling him that his head would be crushed (Gen. 3:14–15).

(2) After telling his followers that he saw Satan fall from heaven, Jesus assured them, "I have given you authority to trample on snakes and scorpions and to overcome all the power of the enemy; nothing will harm you" (Luke 10:19; see also Rom. 16:20).

(3) Just as God had predicted in Genesis 3:14–15, Christ defeated and humiliated Satan and his demonic forces on the cross (Col. 2:15).[17]

(4) Finally, God will cast Satan into the lake of burning sulfur at the final judgment to be tormented forever (Rev. 20:10).

3. The Bible teaches that all have sinned, but God will create a new order for faithful followers of Christ.

a. Sin has always plagued humankind.

(1) Sin has been present in this world from the beginning of human history ever since Adam first disobeyed God in the Garden of Eden (Rom. 5:12–13).

(a) Genesis 3 provides a vivid account of how the first man and first woman sinned.

(b) In addition, God warned their eldest son, Cain, "If you do not do what is right, sin is crouching at your door; it desires to have you, but you must master it" (Gen. 4:7).

(c) Thus the Bible shows that people have not progressed toward sin throughout history; rather, sin has been their condition from the beginning (see Rom. 3:10–12).

(2) Although the Bible describes and lists numerous behavioral sins, God's Word points to our sinful nature as their source (Gal. 5:19–21).

(a) "The sinful nature desires what is contrary to the Spirit" (v. 17), but also "the sinful mind is hostile to God" (Rom. 8:7).

(b) The result is that "your iniquities have separated you from your God" (Isa. 59:2).

(c) Yet the Bible notes that from the beginning a remnant of people has been faithful to God (see Heb. 11).

b. God will not destroy those people who put their faith in Jesus Christ.

(1) Although God will consume the present creation, he will create a new heaven and earth that will endure forever.

(a) Peter described this transition this way:

"By [God's] word the present heavens and earth are reserved for fire, being kept for the day of judgment and destruction of ungodly men.... That day will bring about the destruction of the heavens by fire, and the elements will melt in the heat. But in keeping with his promise we are looking forward to a new heaven and a new earth, the home of righteousness" (2 Peter 3:7, 12–13).

---

[17]"The powers and authorities" in Colossians 2:15 is a Pauline phrase in reference to "the spiritual forces of evil" (Eph. 6:12).

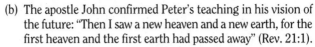

(b) The apostle John confirmed Peter's teaching in his vision of the future: "Then I saw a new heaven and a new earth, for the first heaven and the first earth had passed away" (Rev. 21:1).

(c) Moreover, the prophet Isaiah disclosed not only God's vow to fashion a new order—"Behold, I will create new heavens and a new earth" (Isa. 65:17)—but also God's promise to reserve this new order for his people: "'As the new heavens and the new earth that I make will endure before me,' declares the LORD, 'so will your name and descendants endure'" (66:22).

(2) The Bible reveals that believers in Christ will not experience suffering and death in this new order.

(a) Isaiah declared God's promise that "he will swallow up death forever. The Sovereign LORD will wipe away the tears from all faces" (Isa. 25:8; see also 65:19).

(b) John noted in his vision of heaven that believers in the new heaven and earth "will be his people, and God himself will be with them and be their God. He will wipe every tear from their eyes. There will be no more death or mourning or crying or pain, for the old order of things has passed away" (Rev. 21:3–4).

II. Absolute Truth

A. *The Hindu Position on Absolute Truth Briefly Stated*

1. The Vedas are the highest expression of truth.
2. People who refuse to believe in Hindu scriptures are condemned to hell.
3. All religions are custodians of spiritual truths.
4. No religion can claim that its teachings on truth are absolute.

B. *Arguments Used by Hindus to Support Their Position on Absolute Truth*

1. The Vedas are the highest expression of truth.

a. According to Radhakrishnan, "The Veda, the wisdom, is the accepted name for the highest spiritual truth of which the human mind is capable."[18]

b. Paramahansa Yogananda, a popular Hindu teacher in the West, taught, "Vedic truth, as all truth, belongs to the Lord and not to India. The rishis [ancient sages in India], whose minds were pure receptacles to receive the divine profundities of the Vedas, were members of the human race ... to serve humanity as a whole."[19]

---

[18]Radhakrishnan and Moore, *A Sourcebook in Indian Philosophy,* 615.

[19]Paramahansa Yogananda, *Autobiography of a Yogi* (Los Angeles: Self-Realization Fellowship, 1972), 370, 372.

    c. In other words, the Hindus believe the Vedas convey the purest form of truth for all humanity.

2. People who refuse to believe in Hindu scriptures are condemned to hell.

    a. Any doctrines inconsistent with Vedic teachings are expressions of falsehood.

    b. The Laws of Manu, a sacred manual of Hindu jurisprudence, states, "All those traditions and all those despicable systems of philosophy, which are not based on the Veda, produce no reward after death; for they are declared to be founded on darkness."[20]

    c. Other Hindu scriptures teach that "those sinners who have constantly condemned Vedas, gods or brahmins, those who have ignored the beneficial teachings of Purana and Itihasa . . . all these fall into these hells."[21]

    d. Thus anyone who disagrees with Hindu philosophy—particularly Vedic teachings—is spiritually deluded and condemned to extreme suffering.

3. All religions are custodians of spiritual truths.

    a. Hindu teachers from India have come to the West and extolled the founders and teachings of Western religions.

       (1) Since Hindus acknowledge that truths are always in flux, they can publicly state that all religions are privy to at least some of the deeper truths. Radhakrishnan said, "Hinduism has no fixed creed by which it may be said to stand or fall, for it is convinced that the spirit will outgrow the creed. For the Hindu every religion is true, if only its adherents sincerely and honestly follow it."[22]

       (2) Hindus will say that the holy men and women of every faith have gained unique understanding of truth. "Saints of all religions have attained God-realization," said Yogananda.[23]

    b. Many Hindu masters express special praise for Jesus Christ.

       (1) They claim that Jesus' teaching reflects Vedic philosophy. Sri Yukteswar, spiritual mentor of Yogananda, says, "Quoting the words of the blessed Lord Jesus, I showed that his teachings are in essence one with the revelation of the Vedas."[24]

       (2) They also point out that traditional Christians have misconstrued Christ's message, of which these Hindu masters have a better comprehension. Yogananda said, "Fervently I implored Christ to guide me in divining the true meaning of his words,

---

[20]The Laws of Manu 12.95.
[21]Vamana Purana 12.1.
[22]Radhakrishnan, *Religion and Society* (London: Allen & Unwin, 1959), 53.
[23]Yogananda, *Autobiography of a Yogi*, 96.
[24]Ibid., 392–93.

many of which have been grievously misunderstood for twenty centuries."[25]

4. No religion can claim that its teachings on truth are absolute.

   a. The human mind alone is incapable of comprehending truth.

     (1) Swami Prabhupada, the founder of ISKCON, said what many other Hindu teachers preach: "There is no possibility of understanding the Supreme Absolute Truth simply by speculating, for it lies beyond man's reasoning powers."[26]

     (2) True knowledge of God is beyond the capabilities of the human mind: "We cannot understand the Absolute Truth or the Supreme Person by mental speculation," said Prabhupada.[27]

     (3) Therefore, a person needs a spiritual discipline in order to attain Absolute Truth, which is knowable in every person's self, as is indicated in the Bhagavad-Gita: "There is nothing on earth equal in purity to wisdom. He who becomes perfected by *yoga* finds this of himself, in his self in course of time."[28]

     (4) In other words, each person's understanding of truth is right for himself or herself as long as he or she employs the proper spiritual exercise to discover truth in his or her self.

   b. Since the perception of truth is independent of human reasoning, no religion can dogmatically insist that its view of truth is absolute.

     (1) Radhakrishnan said, "Religion should not be confused with fixed intellectual conceptions, which are all mind-made. Any religion which claims finality and absoluteness desires to impose its own opinions on the rest of the world."[29]

     (2) In other words, all religions that profess to have sole ownership of truth will seek to convert other religious people to their way of thinking, which is utterly wrong to do, particularly since their claim is not possible.

     (3) Moreover, because Hindu scriptures have a right understanding of spiritual reality, they can dismiss the theological views of other religions.

     (4) For instance, the Upanisads state, "This is true even now. Whoso thus knows that he is Brahman, becomes this whole [universe]. Even the gods have not the power to cause him to un-Be, for he becomes their own self. So, whoever reveres any other deity, thinking: 'He is one, and I am another,' does not [rightly] understand."[30]

---

[25]Ibid., 561.

[26]Swami Prabhupada, *Bhagavad-Gita As It Is* (Los Angeles: ISKCON, 1975), 168.

[27]Ibid., *Teachings of Lord Kapila: The Son of Devahuti* (Los Angeles: ISKCON, 1977), 2.

[28]Bhagavad-Gita 4.38.

[29]Radhakrishnan, *Religion and Society*, 52.

[30]Brihadaranyaka Upanisad 1.4.10.

C. Refutation of Arguments Used by Hindus to Support Their Position on Absolute Truth

1. The truth statements of Hindu texts are neither reliable nor compelling.

   a. Unlike Judeo-Christianity, which is consistently theistic throughout its Scriptures, Hindu sacred writings comprise diverse theological systems of thought.

      (1) This diversity is quite evident in Hindu's most sacred texts, the Vedas.

      (2) History of religions scholar David L. Johnson said of the religious focus of the Vedas: "A puzzling thing about *Veda* is that it seems to advocate a number of different religious styles. The early sections advocate prayers and incantations to various gods of nature—gods of the storms, the sun, fire, and mountains. Later sections advocate a priestly religion requiring elaborate rituals of sacrifice and ceremonies of purification. Yet another section insists that rituals and prayers are 'uncertain rafts' upon the ocean of life and that it is necessary for a seeker to renounce the world in favor of a mystical experience found only in isolation."[31]

      (3) The theological view of the Vedas alternates between polytheistic paganism (the belief in and worship of many gods manifested in natural forces) and pantheistic monism (the belief that all is one in god).

      (4) Because absolute truth cannot be self-contradictory, the Vedas are clearly far from adequate as an expression of absolute truth.

   b. Hindu scriptures themselves teach that in the present Kali Age, people will turn away from the Vedas (see Part II, Section I.B.3.a.[4] above).

      (1) Since it is predetermined that all humankind will reject the Vedas and be destroyed, even if the Vedas express absolute truth, why pursue it?

      (2) In contrast, Christian doctrine teaches that those who receive the gospel of Jesus Christ will become God's children and enjoy everlasting fellowship with Christ in his kingdom.

      (3) The appeal of the Christian message seems more compelling than Hindu teachings about the inevitable future desolation of humankind.

2. The Hindu claim that all religions espouse truth is fallacious.

   a. All religions cannot teach absolute truth because their central doctrines are in conflict.

---

[31]David L. Johnson, *A Reasoned Look at Asian Religions* (Minneapolis: Bethany House, 1985), 75.

(1) Consider the fact that different religions often present contradictory teachings on God, salvation, and the soul.

    (a) For example, biblical teachings are theistic, while Vedic teachings are both polytheistic and monistic; the Buddha taught that seeking God is a hindrance to being enlightened to ultimate truth.

    (b) According to Christian doctrine, people are saved only through the grace of God, while in both traditional Hinduism and Buddhism people must accomplish their own salvation.

    (c) Christians also teach that the soul reenters the body at the resurrection, and the person is either received into heaven or sent to hell eternally. Yet Hindus teach the soul is continually reborn until it is absorbed into Brahman; Buddhists teach that there is no soul.

(2) The Dalai Lama, the spiritual leader of the Tibetan Buddhists, says of the differences between Christian and Buddhist doctrines:

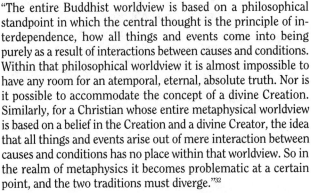

"The entire Buddhist worldview is based on a philosophical standpoint in which the central thought is the principle of interdependence, how all things and events come into being purely as a result of interactions between causes and conditions. Within that philosophical worldview it is almost impossible to have any room for an atemporal, eternal, absolute truth. Nor is it possible to accommodate the concept of a divine Creation. Similarly, for a Christian whose entire metaphysical worldview is based on a belief in the Creation and a divine Creator, the idea that all things and events arise out of mere interaction between causes and conditions has no place within that worldview. So in the realm of metaphysics it becomes problematic at a certain point, and the two traditions must diverge."[32]

b. Hindu scriptures teach that the Buddha spread false religious doctrines.

(1) The Puranas maintain that the Buddha was an avatar of Visnu.

(2) Thus they incorporate the Buddha into their tradition, but undermine Buddhist doctrines by asserting that his purpose was to deceive people.

(3) "At the close of time's twilight, he will become the son of a Jina among the non-Aryans, named Buddha, in order to delude the foes of the gods."[33]

---

[32] His Holiness the Dalai Lama, *The Good Heart: A Buddhist Perspective on the Teachings of Jesus* (Boston: Wisdom, 1996), 81–82.

[33] Garuda Purana 1.12–35.

    (4) Therefore, it is clear that in reality Hindus do not have such a revered respect for other people's beliefs.

3. The value of the human mind is indispensable, and intellectual dogmatism is apparent in Hinduism.

    a. The human mind possesses remarkable abilities.

        (1) The human mind can create inspiring works of art, even those that contain profoundly religious themes, such as Fyodor Dostoyevski's *Crime and Punishment*.

        (2) It can achieve astonishing technological accomplishments, such as journeying to the moon.

        (3) The mind can even perceive the character of God in what it sees in creation (Rom. 1:20).

        (4) Furthermore, non-Christian philosophers such as Cicero noted that "the cultivation of the mind is a kind of food supplied for the soul of man."[34]

        (5) People must use their minds in order to examine and test the veracity of religious statements; for if they don't, they may follow the diabolical leading of any religious leader, such as Jim Jones or David Koresh.

        (6) In his book *Your Mind Matters,* Christian apologist John R. W. Stott speaks of the beneficial powers of the mind. He says, "If we do not use the mind which God has given us, we condemn ourselves to spiritual superficiality and cut ourselves off from many of the riches of God's grace."[35]

    b. It is hypocritical to condemn the exclusive nature of other religious doctrines while exalting one's own dogma as the most perfect expression of Absolute Truth.

        (1) Hindu philosophy is steeped in a mountain of religious texts, both in the form of scripture and commentary, that purport to espouse spiritual truths.

        (2) Thus the belief that its scriptures, particularly the Vedas, are directly received from the gods and hence supremely authoritative is a refined method of intellectualizing Absolute Truth not only so that others will understand but also so that others will believe.

        (3) Therefore, when Hindu teachers or scriptures advocate reverence of Brahman or some other Hindu deities, yet disparage the worship of other gods, they are being just as dogmatic as any zealot of another religion.

---

[34]Cicero, *De Finibus Bonorum et Malorum*, v. 19.
[35]John R. W. Stott, *Your Mind Matters* (Downers Grove, Ill.: InterVarsity Press, 1972), 60.

(4) In effect, they are trying to open the ears of people to their religious doctrines while trying to close the ears of people to the doctrines of other religions.

D. *Arguments Used to Prove the Biblical Doctrine of Absolute Truth to Hindus*

1. The Bible reveals that Jesus is the truth and that he shields Christians from spiritual destruction.

   a. Jesus Christ is the full embodiment of truth.

      (1) According to Scripture, in that "the Word became flesh," Jesus is full of truth (John 1:14).

      (2) In addition, all that Jesus said expressed truth. He repeatedly began his statements by saying, "I tell you the truth" (e.g., Matt. 18:3).[36]

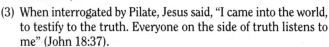

      (3) When interrogated by Pilate, Jesus said, "I came into the world, to testify to the truth. Everyone on the side of truth listens to me" (John 18:37).

      (4) Jesus said, "I am . . . the truth" (John 14:6).

   b. Since Jesus spoke the truth and is the truth, God's faithful listen to Jesus and are under his everlasting care.

      (1) Although Hindu texts warn that those who do not abide by the Vedas will suffer extreme punishment in hell, Jesus promised to protect those who listen to his words.

      (2) Jesus said, "My sheep listen to my voice; I know them, and they follow me. I give them eternal life, and they shall never perish; no one can snatch them out of my hand" (John 10:27–28).

      (3) In addition, one garment of the spiritual armor that protects Christians is "the belt of truth" (Eph. 6:14), which calls to mind "the symbolic clothing of the Messiah"[37] (cf. Isa. 11:5).

      (4) Thus Christians can be confident that they are faithful to the truth and need not fear the threats of other philosophies or religious doctrines.

2. God has revealed his wisdom to Christians, which other people regard as foolishness.

   a. God lavishes *all* wisdom on Christians (Eph. 1:8).

      (1) God's Spirit lives in *all* Christians (Rom. 8:9; 1 Cor. 12:13).

      (2) The Bible refers to God's Spirit as the "Spirit of Truth," who guides Christians into *all* truth (John 16:13).

      (3) Those without God's Spirit will not accept God's truths but will regard them as foolishness (1 Cor. 2:14).

---

[36]Using a concordance, look up the word *truth* in the four Gospels and note how often Jesus used this phrase.

[37]See note under Ephesians 6:14 in the *NIV Study Bible*.

(4) Jesus said, "If you hold to my teaching, you are really my disciples. Then you will know the truth, and the truth will set you free" (John 8:31–32).

b. The wisdom of God was a "mystery" finally revealed in Christ.

(1) Paul said that this "mystery ... has been kept hidden for ages and generations, but is now disclosed to the saints" (Col. 1:26; see also Rom. 16:25–26; 1 Cor. 2:7, 10; Eph. 3:9).

(a) That means God's mystery was not revealed to the sages of other religions, such as the ancient philosophers of India who composed the Vedas.

(b) It means that Christians from the beginning of the church did have knowledge of God's mystery.

(2) Paul said that God's mystery is *Christ,* in whom is all wisdom (Col. 2:2–3; see also 1 Cor. 1:24).

c. Although God revealed the mystery of his wisdom through the public ministry of his Son Jesus Christ, the world, despite its own wisdom, did not understand God's wisdom (1 Cor. 1:21).

(1) The message of Christ's cross is foolishness to those who don't believe in Christ's atonement for sin on the cross (1 Cor. 1:18).

(2) Instead, many non-Christians exchange God's truth for a lie and worship created things (Rom. 1:25), a phenomenon present in Hindu rituals.

d. Therefore, the truth claims in the Bible are incompatible with those of other religions, including Hindu philosophy, because they do not believe Jesus Christ is *the* Son of God, the sole Redeemer of sins. (See more on this in the salvation discussion in section III. below.)

3. People can readily understand God's truth, which should be openly proclaimed.

a. The Bible shows that one need only hear the gospel message in order to understand and believe God's truth.

(1) After Peter preached to a large crowd in Jerusalem, about three thousand believed and accepted his message (Acts 2:14–41).

(2) After Philip explained the Scriptures, an Ethiopian official understood the Good News and believed (8:26–38).

(3) After God opened Lydia's heart to Paul's message about Christ, she became a follower of the Lord (16:13–15).

(4) After Paul and Silas spoke the word of the Lord to the Philippian jailer and his household, they became believers of Christ (16:29–34).

(5) After Paul debated with the Greek philosophers at the Areopagus in Athens, some listeners believed his message (17:22–34).

(6) These examples prove that it is unnecessary to diligently practice a spiritual technique in order to be enlightened to God's

truth. Rather, one's heart must be opened to understand and believe God's truth.

b. The Bible teaches that those who have God's truth must share it with others.

(1) At the end of his public ministry, Jesus commanded his disciples to spread his teachings to all the nations (Matt. 28:18–20).

(2) After Jesus said that his followers will testify about him throughout the world (Acts 1:8–9), Peter made the absolute statement that only through Jesus can a person be saved (4:10, 12).

(3) Because God wants everyone to be saved and have knowledge of the truth—that "there is one God and one mediator between God and men, the man Christ Jesus" (1 Tim. 2:4–5)—Scripture teaches that Christians should "always be prepared to give an answer to everyone" about their faith (1 Peter 3:15).

(4) Therefore, Christians should boldly speak God's absolute truth, being like Paul, who was "not ashamed of the gospel, because it is the power of God for the salvation of everyone who believes (Rom. 1:16).

III. Salvation of the Soul

A. *The Hindu Position on the Salvation of the Soul Briefly Stated*

1. The cycle of death and rebirth is the fate of all unenlightened souls.

2. Those who break free from the cycle of death and rebirth become immortal. That is, deliverance from samsara (cycle of death and rebirth) leads to the immortality of the soul.

3. An enlightened person achieves salvation and perfection through the efforts of one's "self."

4. Ultimate salvation of the soul is total absorption into Brahman.

B. *Arguments Used by Hindus to Support Their Position on the Salvation of the Soul*

1. The cycle of death and rebirth is the fate of all unenlightened souls.

a. *Samsara* is the Hindu term that refers to the cycle of death and rebirth, which Westerners understand as reincarnation.

(1) This doctrine permeates Hindu scriptures, beginning with the Upanisads. The Upanisads are quite clear in their presumption of this belief: "He who in fancy forms desires, because of his desires is born [again] here and there."[38]

(2) The Lord Krisna said to his friend, Arjuna, in the Bhagavad-Gita, "All beings, O Son of Kunti, pass into nature which is My

---

[38]Mundaka Upanisad 3.2.2.

own at the end of the cycle; and at the beginning of the next cycle I send them forth."[39]

b. The law of karma (the Eastern deterministic doctrine of cause and effect) governs the cycle of rebirth and determines the fate of each soul, based on the good and evil acts of previous existences.

(1) The highest state of existence is being one with Brahman, which is the Universal Soul in pure spirit form.

(2) Human souls, which are enmeshed in earthly existences, are ignorant of their true nature and are therefore in bondage to the law of karma and samsara.

(3) Balbir Singh, Hindu scholar, explains,

"What man is in his essential nature transcends what he knows he is. The transcendent element is the soul, the eternal, immutable spiritual principle essentially different from all that is subject to the processes of change, development and decay.... However, human bondage is brought about when the soul comes to be associated with natural desires and passions." Thus, "man subjects himself to a conditioned mode of existence. He renders himself liable to the operation of the law of karma according to which he continues to transmigrate [reincarnate] in order to reap the consequences of his past deeds.... The deeds and their natural consequences force him to be subject to the process of transmigration. He is born, but only to die again. All this, however, because of his ignorance about the truth of his essential nature."[40]

c. Truly spiritual people hold to the doctrine of reincarnation.

(1) Many Hindu leaders point to the early church fathers, such as Origen (c. 185–254), as believers in reincarnation.

(2) Yogananda says, "The early Christian church accepted the doctrine of reincarnation. The truth is that man reincarnates on earth until he has consciously regained his status as a son of God."[41]

2. Those who break free from the cycle of death and rebirth become immortal. That is, deliverance from samsara leads to the immortality of the soul.

a. Hindu scripture is clear about this teaching on the soul: "When the dweller in the body has overcome the gunas [essence of nature] that cause this body, then he is made free from birth and death, from pain and decay: He becomes immortal."[42]

---

[39]Bhagavad-Gita 9.7.

[40]Balbir Singh, *The Philosophy of Upanishads* (Atlantic Highlands, N.J.: Humanities Press, 1983), 90.

[41]Yogananda, *Autobiography of a Yogi,* 199.

[42]Bhagavad-Gita 14.20.

b. Maharishi Mahesh Yogi, the founder of Transcendental Meditation (TM), bases much of his teaching on the Bhagavad-Gita.[43]

(1) He concurs with the Bhagavad-Gita's view of the enlightened soul: "Entry into the Kingdom of Heaven within, getting out of the field of relativity, crossing all limits of creation, and getting to the field of the Creator, is realizing of the Self."[44]

(2) Like many Hindu teachers, Maharishi uses Western terms to convey Eastern thought. In essence, what he is saying is that when one is enlightened to the true nature of one's self, he or she achieves divine immortality, transcends the world of materiality, and becomes one with Brahman.

c. Balbir Singh clarifies the point in drawing a vivid distinction between enlightened and unenlightened souls:

(1) "The true object of our quest is the eternal, immutable, infinite soul. It is in the realization of the soul that one can truly hope to find his supreme good. Such a good alone ever abides."[45]

(2) Meanwhile, "the ignorant will ever hanker after transient desires and their objects, oblivious of the truth about themselves."[46]

3. An enlightened person achieves salvation and perfection through the efforts of one's self.

a. The Hindus teach that bondage to samsara (continuous rebirths in this materialistic world full of evil and suffering) is the supreme curse and that deliverance from this curse can occur only through one's own efforts in attaining self-enlightenment. The Upanisads describe this living hell this way: "In this cycle of existence I am like a frog in a waterless well."[47]

b. Radhakrishnan explains the Hindu concept of personal salvation from samsara this way:

"The souls that have fallen from the higher estate and that now dwell on earth as in a prison pass up and down in their wanderings so that the deeds of an earlier life condition the existence of the following one. The Hindu holds that the goal of spiritual perfection is the crown of a long patient effort. Man grows by countless lives into his divine self-existence."[48]

c. Hindu philosopher Sri Aurobindo notes that this path can be found only in the self: "There can be no real perfection for us except by our inner self."[49]

---

[43]See Yogi, *Maharishi Mahesh Yogi on the Bhagavad-Gita.*

[44]Yogi, *Transcendental Meditation,* 100.

[45]Singh, *The Philosophy of Upanishads,* 91–92.

[46]Ibid., 92.

[47]Maitri Upanisad 1.4.

[48]Radhakrishnan and Moore, *A Sourcebook in Indian Philosophy,* 634.

[49]Sri Aurobindo, *The Life Divine* (New York: Greystone Press, 1949), 931.

4. Ultimate salvation of the soul is total absorption into Brahman.

   a. A person is truly saved when he or she becomes one with Brahman.

   b. The central doctrine of Hindu philosophy asserts that true self-illumination is knowing we are, in fact, Brahman.

   c. Sri Aurobindo said, "The three great declarations of the Upanisads [are] 'I am He,' 'Thou art That, O Svetaketu,' and 'All this is the *Brahman; this Self is the Brahman.*'"[50]

   d. In other words, the pursuit of a true spiritual seeker—such as a yogi—for ultimate truth is, in fact, the quest for ultimate deliverance from this materialistic life and total union with Brahman.

   e. A sacred Hindu text describes the salvation of the soul this way: "When a Yogin pronounces the syllable OM,[51] it reaches the crown of his head. When a Yogin is absorbed in the syllable OM, he becomes eternal.... He becomes one with Brahman.... He wins absorption in Brahman, in the supreme ultimate Self."[52]

C. *Refutation of Arguments Used by Hindus to Support Their Position on the Salvation of the Soul*

1. The transmigration of souls is a belief without empirical support and is not a doctrine of the Christian faith.[53]

   a. Stewart Hackett, a scholar on Eastern philosophy, notes that people who already believe in reincarnation testify to having been reincarnated, but their memories of past lives are confined to their own particular culture and no universal memory exists.[54]

   b. Christian apologist Kurt Van Gorden points out that "almost all so-called memories of reincarnation cases include names of people and places already known in today's world. What we should be searching for is someone who, instead of claiming to be Napoleon, claims to be a formerly unknown tribal leader of an unknown tribe buried in an unknown location, and then find the proofs of such an existence. All attempts, however, have failed miserably."[55]

   c. Atheist philosopher Paul Edwards shows that it is illogical for an impersonal natural law (karma) to mete out rewards and punishments with regard to one's predetermined rebirth (reincarnation) based on one's personal, moral behavior.[56]

---

[50]Ibid., 65.

[51]*Om* is a Vedic syllable that evokes the highest form of Brahman. The meaning of this Sanskrit word is "yes, so be it."

[52]Markandeya Purana 39.6.16.

[53]See Mark Albrecht's fine analysis and refutation of this teaching in *Reincarnation: A Christian Critique of a New Age Doctrine* (Downers Grove, Ill.: InterVarsity Press, 1987).

[54]Stewart Hackett, *Oriental Philosophy* (Madison: University of Wisconsin Press, 1979), 201–2.

[55]Quoted from "Biblical Answers to Reincarnation" (1996), which Van Gorden hands out at his lectures on this subject. The handout can be obtained from Jude 3 Missions, P.O. Box 780, Victorville, CA 92393.

[56]See this and other arguments against reincarnation in Paul Edwards, *Reincarnation: A Critical Examination* (Amherst, NY: Prometheus Books, 1996).

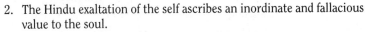
    d. Christian theologian Sydney Cave argues against the Hindu explanation that the laws of karma predetermine a person's character and social standing:

"The large and long established Christian communities of South India have shown how effectively Christian teaching and Christian training can break the power of an evil past, and in these communities many have made an immense advance alike in character and in social standing. Bad heredity and bad environment afford a more adequate explanation for the degradation of the outcaste than does the law of *karma,* and experience shows how successfully spiritual forces, combined with education and an improved environment, can triumph over evils due to bad heredity and environment."[57]

    e. Although Origen and a handful of other Christians conjectured about the preexistence of the soul, the vast majority of Christian theologians, including the early church councils, never endorsed the doctrine of reincarnation. In fact, Origen was "an original and speculative thinker whose works later were often regarded with suspicion in orthodox circles. . . . Some of this teaching was condemned by the Council of Constantinople (553). This included the preexistence of souls."[58]

2. The Hindu exaltation of the self ascribes an inordinate and fallacious value to the soul.

    a. Christian apologist Brooks Alexander provides an astute explanation of this type of attitude toward the self:

      (1) "In its essence it is a kind of self-magnetism—a consistent preference for the claims of self in opposition to those of God. When we spell *Self* with a capital "S" and pursue its spiritual qualities with reverential zeal, we escalate self-exaltation to the specifically religious dimension. In that dimension, our self-absorption becomes self-deification. To choose such values and goals becomes worship, in effect, whether ritualized or not."[59]

      (2) As a result, what is worshiped is far less perfect than the Creator himself, and that is why Alexander calls such wayward homage "the grand lie."[60]

    b. Theologian John Calvin (1509–1564) effectively argued that the soul, which he called "an immortal yet created essence,"[61] is far from perfect in our present sinful state of existence.

[57] Sydney Cave, *Hinduism or Christianity?* (New York: Harper Brothers, 1939), 74–75.

[58] J. D. Douglas, Walter A. Elwell, and Peter Toon, *The Concise Dictionary of the Christian Tradition* (Grand Rapids: Zondervan, 1989), 278.

[59] Brooks Alexander, "The Coming World Religion," *Spiritual Counterfeits Project Journal* (Winter 1984): 21.

[60] Ibid.

[61] John Calvin, *Institutes of the Christian Religion,* ed. John T. McNeill, 2 vols. (Philadelphia: Westminster, 1960), 1:184.

(1) Calvin wrote, "Corruption subsists not in one part only, but that none of the soul remains pure or untouched by that mortal disease [sin]."[62]

(2) Hence, we need only reflect on our inner essence to realize that on our own our natural tendency is to do evil. Observation of our experiences confirms this reality.

(3) Calvin also noted, "Man by nature inclines to deluded self-admiration,"[63] which is why many people zealously insist on exalting the self despite its evident evil nature.

3. It is futile to find salvation or perfection through one's self.

   a. The apostle Paul personally knew how futile it is to resist the temptation to sin on his own.

   (1) He gave a vivid account of how his efforts to be righteous drove him to be an even worse sinner:

   "I know that nothing good lives in me, that is, in my sinful nature. For I have the desire to do what is good, but I cannot carry it out. . . . For in my inner being I delight in God's law; but I see another law at work in the members of my body, waging war against the law of my mind and making me a prisoner of the law of sin at work within my members. What a wretched man I am! Who will rescue me from this body of death?" (Rom. 7:18, 22–24).

   (2) Paul noted that he could not find the strength inside himself to do what is right, but he could find this power only outside himself when he answered his own question: "Thanks be to God—through Jesus Christ our Lord!" (v. 25).

   b. Christian apologist Walter Martin concurs with Paul's assessment about the crippling weakness of our inner self.

   (1) He, too, dismisses self-effort as a way of attaining salvation or deliverance from sin and evil.

   (2) Martin says, "Peace with God is not achieved by looking inside oneself, but by looking up to Him of whom Moses and the prophets did write—Jesus of Nazareth, the Son and Christ of God."[64]

4. The quest to be absorbed into Brahman is spiritually unsatisfying.

   a. Since Brahman is said to be the impersonal Absolute, union with Brahman cannot satisfy people's inner thirst for love from a personal God.

   (1) The ancient psalmists verbalized this thirst: "As the deer pants for streams of water, so my soul pants for you, O God. My soul

---

[62]Ibid., 1:253.

[63]Ibid., 1:242.

[64]Walter Martin, *The Kingdom of the Cults*, rev. ed. (Minneapolis: Bethany House, 1985), 363.

thirsts for God, for the living God" (Ps. 42:1–2), and "O God, you are my God, earnestly I seek you; my soul thirsts for you. . . . Because your love is better than life, my lips will glorify you" (63:1, 3).

(2) Augustine (354–430), bishop of Hippo, echoed this feeling, praying these words to the heavenly Father: "You made us for yourself and our hearts find no peace until they rest in you."[65]

(3) Christian author A. W. Tozer described this inner pleasure of knowing a personal God: "When we lift our inward eyes to gaze upon God we are sure to meet friendly eyes gazing back at us."[66]

b. When people become one with the impersonal Brahman and lose their personal identity, they cannot enjoy those spiritual blessings.

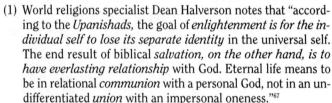

(1) World religions specialist Dean Halverson notes that "according to the *Upanishads,* the goal of *enlightenment is for the individual self to lose its separate identity* in the universal self. The end result of biblical *salvation, on the other hand, is to have everlasting relationship* with God. Eternal life means to be in relational *communion* with a personal God, not in an undifferentiated *union* with an impersonal oneness."[67]

(2) The heavenly Father described in the Bible is a personal God who loves those who love him in an intimate relationship that endures forever.

D. Arguments Used to Prove the Biblical Doctrine of the Salvation of the Soul to Hindus

1. The Bible teaches that each person has one earthly life and that most people experience one physical death.

a. The writer of the epistle to the Hebrews explicitly stated, "Man is destined to die once, and after that to face judgment" (Heb. 9:27).

(1) The two notable exceptions (besides those who are alive at Christ's second coming) recorded in the Bible are Enoch (Gen. 5:24) and Elijah (2 Kings 2:11). Both men evidently did not experience a physical death.

(2) Several people were resurrected from the dead, such as the Shunammite's son (2 Kings 4:34) and Lazarus (John 11:44), but their same bodies died again.

(3) The Bible's point is that a person has only one earthly life.

b. Jesus clearly taught that nothing like the law of karma exists, which determines the condition of a person's life.

---

[65]Saint Augustine, *Confessions* (London: Penguin Books, 1961), 21.

[66]A. W. Tozer, *The Pursuit of God* (Harrisburg, Pa.: Christian Publications, 1948), 92.

[67]Dean C. Halverson, ed., *The Compact Guide to World Religions* (Minneapolis: Bethany House, 1996), 91 (italics in the original).

(1) For example, when Jesus' disciples asked him why a man was born blind, he answered, "Neither this man nor his parents sinned" (John 9:3).

(2) In other words, the man's blindness was not the result of any actions previous to his birth.

c. A proper examination of specific biblical passages precludes the use of these verses as evidence for the reality of reincarnation.

(1) Jesus' declaration that we must be born again (John 3:3) refers to a spiritual birth (vv. 5–8), not a physical rebirth.

(2) Jesus noted that John the Baptist fulfilled the prophetic office of Elijah (Matt. 11:14), not that John was actually the person of Elijah, a notion that John himself denied (John 1:21).

(3) God said to Jeremiah, "Before I formed you in the womb I knew you" (Jer. 1:5). This statement reveals God's omniscience, not that Jeremiah had lived before.

(4) Paul said, "A man reaps what he sows" (Gal. 6:7). Paul was speaking of the actions of current lives and not previous existences, which is clear in a preceding verse in which he urged his readers to test their actions (v. 4).

2. The Bible warns against self-adulation, for only the Lord is worthy of worship.

a. God looks with disfavor on those who exalt themselves, but with favor on those who humble themselves.

(1) Although the Bible condemns the pride of the wealthy and powerful, it is also harsh with those who are poor yet who are overly attentive to themselves.

(2) Jesus pointedly said to the multitude and his own disciples, who lived on the charity of others, "Whoever exalts himself will be humbled, and whoever humbles himself will be exalted" (Matt. 23:12; see also Luke 14:11).

(3) It is the Lord God who humbles and exalts people (1 Sam. 2:7; Ps. 18:27; Ezek. 21:26; Luke 1:52).

(4) God receives only those who are contrite and humble (Isa. 57:15).

(5) In other words, God examines the heart of a person, not one's station in life, to know what is central to that person. "For where your treasure is, there your heart will be also" (Matt. 6:21), and if your treasure is your self, God will surely humble you.

b. Everyone who is an offspring of a woman and a man is permeated with sin.

(1) The Bible repeatedly declares that everyone is a sinner (1 Kings 8:46; 2 Chron. 6:36; Job 14:1, 4; 15:14; Ps. 14:1, 3; 53:1, 3; 143:2; Eccl. 7:20; Rom. 3:9, 23; 5:12; Gal. 3:22; 1 John 1:8, 10).

      (2) Even at the point of conception, people are sinful (Ps. 51:5; see also Job 15:14: Ps. 58:3).

      (3) God's Word notes that the human soul is cursed with sin (Ezek. 18:4; see also Jer. 17:9).

      (4) Jesus said, "No one is good—except God alone" (Mark 10:18; Luke 18:19).

3. The New Testament teaches that no human effort can contribute to one's salvation.

   a. Paul wrote, "For it is by [God's] grace you have been saved, through faith—and this not from yourselves, it is the gift of God—not by works, so that no one can boast" (Eph. 2:8–9).

   b. Not only do we need God to deliver us from sin, but also nothing we have previously done is worthy of Christ's sacrificing his life in order to save us. Paul said that Christ "saved us, not because of righteous things we had done, but because of his mercy" (Titus 3:5).

   c. Therefore, none of our efforts in the past, present, or future can ever empower us to escape from sin, evil, and death. Paul said, "You see, at just the right time, when we were still *powerless,* Christ died for the ungodly" (Rom. 5:6, italics added)—which we all were and will continue to be unless we receive Christ as our Lord and Savior.

4. God's Word reveals that salvation can come only through Jesus Christ.

   a. New Testament doctrine insists that Jesus completed the work of salvation once and for all when he died on the cross to redeem people from their sins (Heb. 7:27; 9:12; 10:12, 14; 1 Peter 3:18).

      (1) The apostle Peter declared, "It is by the name of Jesus Christ of Nazareth.... Salvation is found in no one else, for there is no other name under heaven given to men by which we must be saved" (Acts 4:10, 12).

      (2) Jesus announced, "I am the way and the truth and the life. No one comes to the Father except through me" (John 14:6).

   b. Salvation in Christ affects believers in many critical ways.

      (1) Jesus Christ "purifies us from all sin" (1 John 1:7; see also 1 Cor. 6:11; Col. 3:13; Titus 2:13–14; 1 John 2:2; Rev. 1:5).

      (2) When God forgave us our sins because of Jesus' act of atonement, he "reconciled us to himself through Christ" (2 Cor. 5:18; see also Rom. 5:9–11; Col. 1:21–22).

      (3) The benefits of being saved in Jesus Christ include everlasting life (John 3:16, 36; 6:40, 46–47; 10:28; Rom. 6:23; Titus 3:7), a place in heaven (John 14:1–4; 2 Cor. 5:1; 1 Peter 1:3–4), and perfection (Heb. 10:14).

IV. Jesus Christ

A. *The Hindu Position on Jesus Christ Briefly Stated*

   1. Christ did not suffer.
   2. Jesus was not perfect.
   3. Jesus Christ was one of many great holy men.
   4. Highest reverence should be offered to Brahman, who is the greatest among all the gods.

B. *Arguments Used by Hindus to Support Their Position on Jesus Christ*

   1. Christ did not suffer.

      a. It is absurd to view Christ as a sufferer, because he was a spiritually enlightened man beyond physical pain.

      b. Although Hindu scriptures do not comment on Jesus Christ, contemporary Hindu leaders have much to say about him.

      (1) One view is that Christ did not actually suffer.

      (2) Maharishi Mahesh Yogi, who boasts of a great following, stated, "I don't think Christ ever suffered or Christ could suffer.... It's a pity that Christ is talked of in terms of suffering."[68]

   2. Jesus was not perfect.

      a. Like all humans, Jesus had moral imperfections.

      b. Most Hindu swamis and gurus have high praise for the life and teachings of Jesus Christ, but they do not acknowledge that he was sinless and morally perfect.

      c. Radhakrishnan points to unbridled anger as a major flaw in Jesus' character:

      "No man on earth has ever maintained spiritual poise all through his life. The Jesus who declared that men must not resist evil if they are to become the sons of the Father who makes his sun shine upon good men and bad, and his rain to fall upon the just and the unjust, was the same Jesus who cursed the fig-tree and drove the tradesmen from the temple."[69]

   3. Jesus Christ was one of many great holy men.

      a. All religions have given spiritual masters to the world, and Jesus Christ was only one of them.

      b. Although many Hindu leaders often express their admiration for Jesus as a spiritual teacher and an enlightened man, they recognize him neither as the one and only Savior of humankind nor as the unique Son of God.

      c. They assign Christ to an elite group of holy people who are all as spiritually remarkable as he was.

---

[68]Yogi, *Meditations of Maharishi Mahesh Yogi* (New York: Bantam, 1968), 123-24.
[69]Radhakrishnan and Moore, *A Sourcebook in Indian Philosophy,* 634.

d. Yogananda says, "The great masters of India mold their lives by the same godly ideals that animated Jesus. Freemen all, lords of themselves, the Yogi-Christs of India are part of the immortal fraternity."[70]

e. Some Hindus go so far as to say that there were greater holy men than Jesus. For example, Bali Mardan Maharaj, president of the New York ISKCON center, once stated, "Prabhupada [founder of the Hare Krishna movement, whom followers believe to be the incarnation of Krisna] was a world-genius, greater than Jesus."[71]

4. Highest reverence should be offered to Brahman, who is the greatest among all the gods.

   a. Although some Hindu teachers will acknowledge that Jesus might have been an avatar (a human incarnation of one of the gods), they assign Jesus a status lower than Brahman's in their pantheon of deities.

   b. Their exalted, and for many of them singular, reverence toward Brahman is consistent with the teachings of Hindu holy texts. For instance, the ancient Vedas teach, "Whoso in Man knows Brahman, knows the highest Lord.... Whereas the gods who Brahman know revere Brahman as the highest, best."[72]

C. Refutation of Arguments Used by Hindus to Support Their Position on Jesus Christ

1. Even non-Christian accounts report that Jesus suffered.

   a. The first-century historian Flavius Josephus (A.D. 37–post 100), a Jewish general who was in no way sympathetic to the Christian sect, alluded to Jesus' execution, in his *Antiquities* (18.3.3, 20–21).

   b. Roman orator and historian Publius Cornelius Tacitus (A.D. 55–117) made a similar reference to Jesus in his *Annuals* (1544).

   c. Jesus' suffering is mentioned in a third ancient work, *Life of Claudius* (25).

2. Jesus' anger was righteous indignation, which was consistent with God's anger.

   a. Anger is not necessarily an evil emotion.

      (1) When venom toward another person fuels one's anger, then that anger is wrong and ungodly.

      (2) However, when anger is a controlled response to evil and wickedness, then that anger is appropriate and justified.

   b. God himself has shown anger and will do so until the Day of Judgment.

---

[70]Yogananda, *Autobiography of a Yogi,* 195–96.
[71]Faye Levine, *The Strange World of the Hare Krishnas* (New York: Fawcett, 1974), 69.
[72]Atharva Veda 10.7.17, 24.

49

(1) For example, when human wickedness was universal and exceedingly wanton, God decided to wipe out humankind, and he did so with the Flood (Gen. 6:5–7).

(2) On the Day of Judgment, God will punish "with everlasting destruction" those who have turned away from him (2 Thess. 1:8–9).

c. Hindu scriptures describe anger even in their gods.

(1) In homage to the great Hindu god Indra, the Rg Veda proclaims, "When heightened in his ire his indignation shatters the firm and breaks the strong in pieces."[73]

(2) The Vamana Purana describes an extremely angry exchange between Brahma and Siva, two of the three most important Hindu gods (trimurti).[74]

d. Radhakrishnan's examples of Jesus' anger are misinterpreted.

(1) After Jesus cursed the fig tree because it bore no fruit, he explained to his disciples how powerful is a prayer said in faith (Matt. 21:18–22; Mark 11:12–14, 20–25).

(a) The text does not indicate that Jesus was angry and that he hurt a human being, but rather that he withered a *tree*.

(b) Jesus was making a point to his disciples about prayer, which he ended with a call to his followers to forgive people who have wronged them (Mark 11:25).

(2) After he saw how the greedy moneychangers had defiled the temple area with their presence, Jesus overturned their tables and drove them out (Matt. 21:12–13; Mark 11:15–17; Luke 19:45–46; John 2:13–16).

(a) Jesus was obviously upset that avarice had entered his Father's house.

(b) Biblical scholar Leon Morris comments on the apostle John's account: "The action of Jesus gave evidence of a consuming zeal for the house of God. We should not miss the way this incident fits in with John's aim of showing Jesus to be the Messiah. All his actions imply a special relationship with God. They proceed from his messianic vocation."[75]

(c) Jesus was right to feel angry, and he showed his anger with righteous indignation; it was not a moral defect in his character.

3. Only Jesus is worthy of the title of "Christ."

a. The term *Christ* is specifically designated for Jesus of Nazareth.

(1) The Greek word *Christos* means "anointed."

---

[73]Rg Veda 1.6.
[74]Vamana Purana 2.23–34.
[75]Leon Morris, *The Gospel According to John*, rev. ed., NICNT Series (Grand Rapids: Eerdmans, 1995), 172.

(2) New Testament writers repeatedly referred to Jesus as the Christ because God had anointed his Son to be the Messiah— the Savior of the world.

(3) Jesus atoned for the sins of God's people by bearing their sins on the cross and taking their punishment upon himself through his death.

(4) Hence, Jesus reconciled God's people to the heavenly Father through the sacrifice of his sinless life.

(5) Biblical scholar F. F. Bruce explains, "The humanity of Christ is shared by him with all mankind. But ours is 'sinful flesh', because sin has established a bridgehead in our life by means of which it dominates the human situation. Christ came in real flesh—he lived and died in a 'body of flesh' (Colossians 1:22)— but he did not come in 'sinful flesh', because sin gained no foothold in his life; he is said therefore to have come 'in the *likeness* of sinful flesh', so that, when he presented his life as a sin-offering, God thus 'condemned sin in the flesh' (Romans 8:3)—passed the death-sentence on it by virtue of the sinless humanity of Christ."[76]

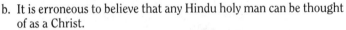

b. It is erroneous to believe that any Hindu holy man can be thought of as a Christ.

(1) Although he had a false understanding of the character of Christ, Radhakrishnan himself admitted that no one has lived a perfect life (see IV.B.2.c above).

(2) Neither Hindu scriptures nor Hindu teachers have ever asserted that a particular holy man or woman has died for the sins of the world. As we have seen, it is up to the individual seeker to attain perfection for oneself (see III.B.3 above).

(3) Therefore, since Hindu saints have not fulfilled the divine office of Christ as Jesus has, Hindus cannot rightfully refer to the saints in their religion as "Christs," or even "Yogi-Christs" as Yogananda has done.

4. Whereas Brahman is not exclusively preeminent within Hinduism, Jesus Christ is within Christianity.

a. Although Brahman is often exalted in Hindu literature, the Hindu holy texts do not consistently uphold Brahman as being preeminent in the Hindu pantheon.

(1) Indra is the most prominent god in the early Vedic scriptures, though the fire god, Agni, emerged as the primary recipient of oblations from Brahmin priests during their sacrificial rituals.

(2) Rama, an avatar (incarnation) of the god Visnu, is the heroic figure in the epic Ramayana.

---

[76]F. F. Bruce, *Paul: Apostle of the Heart Set Free* (Grand Rapids: Eerdmans, 1977), 204–5.

(3) Krisna, another avatar of Visnu, is the central character of the Mahabharata, particularly of the Bhagavad-Gita, a section of that massive epic.

(4) Siva appears as the most significant god in some of the Puranas, as does Visnu.

(5) Even today followers of Krisna or Siva contend that their god is the supreme god of the universe.[77]

b. Jesus Christ, without question or rival, is preeminent within the Christian faith.

(1) He is the central focus of all twenty-seven books of the New Testament.

(2) All the creeds of the church, from the Apostles' Creed onward, give exclusive homage to Jesus Christ as God and Savior.

(3) Orthodox Christians from the time of Jesus' public ministry have confessed Jesus Christ as their only Lord and Master.

(4) World religions historian John B. Noss says, "The story of Christianity is the story of a religion which has sprung from the faith that in its founder God was made manifest in the flesh and dwelt among men. In the belief that Jesus is the clearest portrayal of the character of God all the rest of Christian doctrine is implied."[78]

c. Hence, Christians can have unreserved confidence that both Scripture and tradition will support their belief in the supremacy of Jesus Christ; yet such a conviction on the part of Hindus is reasonably suspect, considering the polytheistic nature of their holy texts and independent movements within their own religion.

D. Arguments Used to Prove the Biblical Doctrine of Jesus Christ to Hindus

1. The New Testament discloses how Jesus suffered grievously in many ways (see Mark 8:31).

a. Jesus suffered physically.

(1) All four Gospels relate how the Roman soldiers brutally beat Jesus and finally crucified him on the cross (Matt. 27:27–35; Mark 15:16–25; Luke 23:33; John 19:1–2, 16–18).

(2) Biblical scholar William Barclay says of the apostle John's description of Jesus' horrible crucifixion experience: "He brings us face to face with the human suffering of Jesus. . . . he wished to show that Jesus was really a human being, and really underwent the pain and the agony of the Cross. John goes out of his way to stress the real humanity, the real manhood, and the real suffering of Jesus."[79]

---

[77]See Cornelia Dimmitt and J. A. van Buitenen's quote in Part I, Section II.D.1.b.

[78]John B. Noss, *Man's Religions*, rev. ed. (New York: Macmillan, 1956), 555.

[79]William Barclay, *The Gospel of John*, 2 vols. (Philadelphia: Westminster, 1956), 2:300–301.

(3) When Jesus fasted for forty days in the wilderness and was tempted by the devil, he suffered hunger pangs just as any other human being would (Matt. 4:2; Luke 4:2).

b. Jesus suffered grief for others.

(1) After his friend Lazarus died, Jesus approached the burial tomb and was deeply moved and troubled at the sight of people's weeping. In response, "Jesus wept" (John 11:35).

(2) Jesus expressed deep grief for the Jewish people who had rejected their God, likening himself to a mother hen who longs to comfort her chicks under her wings (Matt. 23:37; Luke 13:34).

c. Jesus suffered scorn and rejection from others.

(1) The prophet Isaiah said of Jesus, "He was despised and rejected by men, a man of sorrows, and familiar with suffering" (Isa. 53:3).

(2) This was particularly evident when people insulted, sneered, and mocked Jesus while he died on the cross (Matt. 27:39, 41; Mark 15:29–31; Luke 23:35–37).

(3) Peter, one of Jesus' closest friends, denied him (Luke 22:59–61).

d. Jesus suffered the worse kind of pain when he felt abandoned by God on the cross as he bore the sins of humanity (1 Peter 2:21, 24).

(1) Jesus cried out, "My God, my God, why have you forsaken me?" (Matt. 27:46; Mark 15:34).

(2) What suffering can be worse than feeling abandoned by your heavenly Father? Obviously, none.

2. The Bible indicates that Jesus was and is perfect in every way.

a. Although Jesus is a man, he was and is sinless.

(1) Jesus the Son of God was "tempted in every way, just as we are—yet was without sin" (Heb. 4:15).

(2) In fact, he "had no sin" (2 Cor. 5:21).

b. As our high priest, Jesus "is holy, blameless, pure, set apart from sinners, exalted above the heavens" (Heb. 7:26).

c. God's Son "has been made perfect forever" (Heb. 7:28) in that he faced temptation throughout his life without ever succumbing to sin by always being in perfect obedience to his heavenly Father (2:10; 5:8–9).

3. The Bible teaches that Jesus is the only Christ.

a. The apostle John pointedly stated, "Who is the liar? It is the man who denies that Jesus is the Christ" (1 John 2:22).

b. No one else is the Christ, who has reconciled humankind with God.

(1) Jesus said about himself, "You have one Teacher, the Christ" (Matt. 23:10).

(2) The apostle Paul wrote to the Christians in Corinth, "There is but one Lord, Jesus Christ" (1 Cor. 8:6; see also Eph. 4:5).

(3) Paul believed that God's grace came by "the one man, Jesus Christ" (Rom. 5:15); for "through the obedience of the one man the many will be made righteous" (v. 19).

(4) Paul also noted in his epistles that he was convinced that "one died for all" (2 Cor. 5:14) and that there is "one mediator between God and men" (1 Tim. 2:5).

  c. Scripture alerts believers to those who distort the biblical teaching about Christ.

(1) Jesus warned his followers, "If anyone says to you, 'Look, here is the Christ!' or, 'Look, there he is!' do not believe it" (Mark 13:21; see also Matt. 24:23).

(2) Paul reminded his friend Timothy, "Watch your life and doctrine closely" (1 Tim. 4:16).

4. Scripture clearly shows that Jesus Christ is the divine ruler over all creation.

  a. Jesus Christ is God.

(1) The apostle Peter declared Jesus to be his "God and Savior" (2 Peter 1:1).

(2) The apostle Paul proclaimed Jesus to be his "great God" (Titus 2:13).

(3) Paul further said, "For in Christ all the fullness of the Deity lives in bodily form" (Col. 2:9).

(4) Speaking of Jesus, the apostle John said that "the Word was God" and "the Word became flesh" (John 1:1, 14).

(5) When he saw Jesus' resurrected body, the apostle Thomas exclaimed, "My Lord and my God" (John 20:28).

(6) The heavenly Father called his Son "God" (Heb. 1:8).

  b. Jesus Christ reigns victoriously over all.

(1) After God raised Jesus from the dead, he seated Jesus "far above all rule and authority, power and dominion" now and forever (Eph. 1:21).

(2) "God exalted him to the highest place and gave him the name that is above every name, that at the name of Jesus every knee should bow, in heaven and on earth and under the earth, and every tongue confess that Jesus Christ is Lord, to the glory of God the Father" (Phil. 2:9–11).

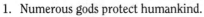

V. God

A. The Hindu Position on God Briefly Stated

1. Numerous gods protect humankind.
2. Brahman is the creator of the world.
3. True enlightenment is knowing that we are one with god. That is, we are god.

B. Arguments Used by Hindus to Support Their Position on God

1. Numerous gods protect humankind.

   a. The Hindu pantheon includes not only Brahman, the creator; Visnu, the preserver; and Siva, the destroyer; but also Indra, the god of the thunderstorm; Agni, the god of fire; Kali, the mother goddess and consort of Siva; Brhaspati, the god of wisdom; Surya, the sun-god; Varuna, the god of cosmic order; and many more.

   b. Hindus believe that these deities are supernatural guardians over those who faithfully worship them.

   c. The Rg Veda expresses that belief in the following invocation: "That the gods ever may be with us for our gain, our guardians day by day unceasing in their care. May the auspicious favour of the gods be ours, on us descend the bounty of the righteous gods. The friendship of the gods have we devoutly sought; so may the gods extend our life that we may live."[80]

2. Brahman is the creator of the world.

   a. Brahman, or Krisna, was the beginning of all things.

   b. The Upanisads claim, "In the beginning this [universe] was Brahman alone. . . . So, whoever reveres any other deity, thinking: 'He is one, and I am another,' does not [rightly] understand."[81]

   c. The Bhagavad-Gita asserts, "Lord Krisna declared, 'Know that all beings have their birth in this. I am the origin of all this world and its dissolution as well. There is nothing whatever that is higher than I. . . . I am the syllable Aum [OM][82] in all the Vedas. . . . I am not in them [all beings]; they are in Me.'"[83]

   d. In any case, Hindus believe that the origin of this world has its source in one of their gods.

3. True enlightenment is knowing that we are one with god. That is, we are god.

   a. In the Upanisads appears the central doctrine of modern Hindu philosophy.

---

[80]Rg Veda 1.89.1–2.
[81]Brhadaranyaka Upanisad 1.4.10.
[82] On *om,* see III.B.4.e and note 51 above.
[83]Bhagavad-Gita 7.6-8, 12.

(1) The Chandogya Upanisad reads, "They become the ocean itself. . . . Whatever they are in this world, whether tiger, or lion, or wolf, or boar, or worm, or fly, or gnat, or mosquito, that they become. That which is the finest essence—this whole world has that as its self. That is Reality. That is *Atman.* That art thou, Svetaketu."[84]

(2) "That" is Brahman (the Universal Soul or the absolute, undifferentiated reality), and "thou" is Atman (the soul or self of the individual person).

(3) In other words, "That art thou" means "Brahman is you," or even more simply, "I am god."

   b. Such realization is the most perfect understanding of Absolute Truth.

(1) Absolute Truth is achieved by practicing spiritual disciplines (such as yogic techniques) that help an individual seeker explore the hidden meaning of the inner self.

(2) Krisna reveals to Arjuna in the Bhagavad-Gita, "God is flawless and the same in all. . . . He who finds his happiness within, his joy within, and likewise his light only within, that yogin becomes divine."[85]

C. *Refutation of Arguments Used by Hindus to Support Their Position on God*

  1. Christian theism is free from the conundrums evident in Hindu polytheism.

    a. The Hindu conception of god is flawed because of the contradictions between its diverse statements about god.

(1) Among Hindu sacred texts, the Hindus offer their highest reverence for Vedic scriptures.

(2) Radhakrishnan says, "The Hindus look back to the Vedic period as the epoch of their founders. The Veda, the wisdom, is the accepted name for the highest spiritual truth of which the human mind is capable. It is the work of the *rsis* or the seers. The truths of the *rsis* are not evolved as the result of logical reasoning or systematic philosophy but they are the products of spiritual intuition, *drsti* or vision. The *rsis* are not so much the authors of the truths recorded in the Vedas as the seers who were able to discern the eternal truths by raising their life-spirit to the plane of the universal spirit."[86]

(3) The Rg Veda, however, verbalizes its highest praise to the god Indra, whose supernatural attributes are associated with the

---

[84]Chandogya Upanisad 6.10.1–3.
[85]Bhagavad-Gita 5.19, 24.
[86]Radhakrishnan and Moore, *A Sourcebook in Indian Philosophy,* 615–16.

primal forces of nature, and yet for centuries Hindus have not accorded Indra the prominence the Rg Veda has.

(4) The Hindus argue that their comprehension of the Absolute has evolved so that they now understand that Brahman, as the impersonal Absolute, or Krisna, as a personal manifestation of the Absolute, provides a clearer understanding of the godhead.

(5) Radhakrishnan says, "Hinduism has no fixed creed by which it may be said to stand or fall, for it is convinced that the spirit will outgrow the creed."[87]

(6) Radhakrishnan's two statements are contradictory: Within Hindu theology, either the Rg Veda expresses a truth about god that is directly from god and therefore immutable, or later Hindu perceptions of the divine provide better insights about the true meaning of the godhead. One cannot have it both ways, which is a major flaw in a polytheistic system such as Hinduism.

(7) In addition, to say that the Hindu comprehension of Absolute Reality (Brahman) has evolved to higher levels of understanding contradicts the Puranas, which teach that humankind is currently in the age of ignorance (Kali Yuga) and hurling further away from truth.

b. By contrast, the Christian faith is devoted not only to one God but also to a personal God.

(1) Hence, people can know this same one God and have a relationship with this God.

(2) Christian apologist James Sire says, "To be a Christian theist is not just to have an intellectual world view; it is to be personally committed to the infinite-personal Lord of the Universe. And it leads to an examined life that is well worth living."[88]

(3) Having such a relationship with one God leaves no room for deities' competing for human worship, as the Puranas depict in the rivalry among Brahman, Visnu, and Siva.[89]

2. The Hindu explanation of human ignorance calls into question the belief that Brahman is the preeminent creator of the world.

a. According to modern Hindu thought, Brahman is ultimate reality and has manifested himself as consciousness (*purusa*) and as material form (*prakrti*).

(1) Hence Brahman is the essence of all reality, and therefore people can worship Brahman in whatever form best helps them on the path to self-illumination.

---

[87]Radhakrishnan, *Religion and Society,* 53.
[88]James W. Sire, *The Universe Next Door,* 2d ed. (Downers Grove, Ill.: InterVarsity Press, 1988), 219.
[89]See Kurma Purana 1.25.64–95.

(2) One of the most captivating forms of Brahman is as Krisna, whom devotees believe is the first cause and the power behind all that happens in our world.

b. Because ignorance obscures people's realization that their souls are also manifestations of Brahman, they are in bondage to rebirth and perpetual suffering.

c. The belief that all is Brahman and that human ignorance exists poses a severe problem for the Hindu. David Johnson asks several troubling questions that bring to light this problem:

"If the world is but one vast spirit, why do we share the ignorant conclusion that it is made up of many things? Where did this conclusion come from? What is its cause? Who is ignorant? Who makes the mistake? Is Brahman (ultimate reality) making the mistake? Is it being said that the one vast spirit has made a mental error by suggesting to me that I am an individual? Has Brahman erred? How could what is described as ultimate 'intelligence' make a mistake?"[90]

d. Because Brahman (or whatever form he takes to manifest himself as god to people) is said to be not only the First Cause of all things but also one with all things, invariably one must attribute the origin of ignorance to him, as Johnson suggests. Therefore, to say that Brahman is Absolute Truth is illogical since he is the source of ignorance.

e. Judeo-Christian teaching avoids this doctrinal problem by asserting that God, being separate from his creation, gave freedom to both angels and humankind's first parents, who disobeyed him; therefore their disobedience is the first cause of evil, suffering, and death.

3. Self-worship is self-deceptive and idolatrous.

a. Christian writer G. K. Chesterton said, "Of all conceivable forms of enlightenment, the worst is what these people call the Inner Light. Of all horrible religions the most horrible is the worship of the god within."[91]

b. To try to convince Hindus of the fallacy of this belief is usually quite difficult.

(1) There is some truth to this belief; after all, God created man in his image (Gen. 1:27). This self-deception would have little seductive power if there were no validity to it.

(2) What occurs is that people deceive themselves about who they are and who God is by worshiping God's image within themselves instead of worshiping God who bestowed his divine image

[90]Johnson, *A Reasoned Look at Asian Religions,* 97.
[91]G. K. Chesterton, *Orthodoxy* (Garden City, N.Y.: Image Books, 1959), 76.

within them. The very radiance of God's image within them blinds them to the Creator whom it ought to reveal to them.

c. Another difficulty in conveying the truth about the Creator to Hindu believers is that they reject any basis for debating their beliefs since they believe these beliefs transcend the human ability to reason.

(1) They assert that such declarations as "That art thou," "Atman is Brahman," "All is one," and "I am god" are not theoretical propositions, but expressions of spiritual experiences achieved in a state of God-consciousness in which all distinctions are dissolved into a single, undifferentiated unity.

(2) Brooks Alexander states, "This form of self-deception is appealing to a humanity sunk in its own self-magnetism. As a means of unifying a broken existence, it 'works,' for obvious reasons. As a means of dealing with conscience, guilt, and judgment, it is the ultimate vanishing act: there is no one to judge if there is no one at all!"[92]

D. Arguments Used to Prove the Biblical Doctrine of God to Hindus

1. The Bible teaches that there is but one God.

a. From the beginning of the Judeo-Christian Scriptures and early in the history of the Jewish people, God insisted that he alone is God, declaring, "There is no god besides me" (Deut. 32:39).

b. God also said, "Before me no god was formed, nor will there be one after me" (Isa. 43:10). Of course, nothing existed before God, nor will God cease to exist, since he is eternal (Gen. 21:33; Ps. 90:2; Isa. 40:28; Rom. 16:26), but this statement was God's way to vividly impress upon his people that only he is God.

c. Moses told God's people, "Acknowledge and take to heart this day that the LORD is God in heaven above and on the earth below. There is no other" (Deut. 4:39; see also v. 35; 1 Kings 8:60; 2 Kings 19:19; Ps. 86:10; Neh. 9:6).

d. Paul reminded Christians "that an idol is nothing at all in the world and that there is no God but one" (1 Cor. 8:4).

e. God mocked those who put their trust and security in gods that in fact do not exist: "Where then are the gods you made for yourselves? Let them come if they can save you when you are in trouble!" (Jer. 2:28).

2. Scripture reveals that God is the Creator.

a. God created the spiritual and the physical realms as well as humankind.

(1) The first statement in the Bible declares, "In the beginning God created the heavens and the earth" (Gen. 1:1).

---

[92]Brooks Alexander, "Occult Philosophy and Mystical Experience," *Spiritual Counterfeits Project Journal* (Winter 1984): 18.

(2) From the beginning to the end of the Bible this fact is proclaimed (see Gen. 14:19; Rev. 4:11; 10:6).

(3) Over and over again God tells his people, "I am the LORD, and there is no other; apart from me there is no God.... It is I who made the earth and created mankind upon it.... And there is no God apart from me, a righteous God and a Savior; there is none but me.... I am God, and there is no other; I am God, and there is none like me" (Isa. 45:5, 12, 21; 46:9).

(4) God created not only the physical form of humanity, but also their souls: "You created my inmost being," said the psalmist (Ps. 139:13).

b. When God created humankind, he did not create man and woman evil.

(1) "Sin entered the world through one man [Adam], and death through sin, and in this way death came to all men, because all sinned" (Rom. 5:12).

(2) In other words, "death came through a man, ... in Adam all die" (1 Cor. 15:21–22).

(3) Adam and Eve had the choice either to obey or to disobey God's commands; they chose to disobey, which brought humankind to ruin (see Gen. 3).

c. When Paul spoke to the philosophers in Athens, he spoke not only of God's creative attributes but also of God's provision, through the resurrection of his Son Jesus Christ, for bridging the breach between himself and human beings.

"The God who made the world and everything in it is the Lord of heaven and earth and does not live in temples built by hands. And he is not served by human hands, as if he needed anything, because he himself gives all men life and breath and everything else. From one man he made every nation of men, that they should inhabit the whole earth; and he determined the times set for them and the exact places where they should live. God did this so that men would seek him and perhaps reach out for him and find him, though he is not far from each one of us.... now he commands all people everywhere to repent. For he has set a day when he will judge the world with justice by the man he appointed. He has given proof of this to all men by raising him from the dead" (Acts 17:24–27, 30–31).

3. God's Word clearly identifies who God is.

a. God is the great "I AM," and he is one.

(1) When Moses asked God who he should say had sent him, God replied, "I AM WHO I AM. This is what you are to say to the Israelites, 'I AM has sent me'" (Exod. 3:14).

(2) The Jewish confession of faith (Shema) came soon afterward and remains to this day: "Hear, O Israel: The LORD our God, the LORD is one" (Deut. 6:4).

(3) Jesus affirmed this confession during his public ministry, saying that the most important commandment is this: "Hear, O Israel, the Lord our God, the Lord is one" (Mark 12:29).

b. Man is not God.

(1) In Isaiah 46–47 God condemned Babylon for usurping his name and his identity as God. This idolatry can be seen in the repeated statements that include the phrase "I am." Babylon spoke of itself as "I am" when in fact this designation belonged to God alone.

(2) The prophet Ezekiel wrote, "In the pride of your heart you say, 'I am a god; I sit on the throne of a god in the heart of the seas.' But you are a man and not a god, though you think you are as wise as a god" (Ezek. 28:2).

(3) Furthermore, Scripture states directly, "God is not a man" (Num. 23:19).

c. The key to avoiding self-idolatry is provided in both Moses and Jesus' words that follow the Shema: "Love the Lord your God with all your heart and with all your soul and with all your mind and with all your strength" (Mark 12:30; see also Deut. 6:5).

Part III: Witnessing Tips

I. Classification of Hindu Groups in North America

A. *Profile of Individual Groupings*

1. North Americans who dabble with Hindu practices but not for religious reasons;
2. North Americans who are involved with Hindu practices and study Hindu philosophy to enhance their spiritual life;
3. North Americans who have devoted their entire life to a Hindu organization;
4. Asian Indians in North America or Indian Americans whose religious orientation is Hindu.

B. *Representative Groups*

1. North Americans who have been initiated into the practice of TM;
2. North Americans who profess to be adherents of Hinduism;
3. North Americans who are members of ISKCON (the Hare Krishna movement);
4. Asian Indians or Asian-Indian Americans who consider themselves Hindus (by far, the most important group when considering evangelism because of their numbers and actual contact with Christians).

II. Transcendental Meditation

A. *Who are they?*

1. According to TM flyers and advertisements, TM organizations have initiated about 4 million people worldwide, of which about half are in North America.
2. A very small percentage of these people currently have ties with a TM organization (see below under "Western Adherents of Hinduism").
3. Many TM initiates were spiritual seekers who later joined other groups that are openly religious.
4. Most TM initiates tried this practice merely to relieve stress and attain inner tranquility, and have since abandoned this practice.
5. Nevertheless, the Maharishi Vedic University programs are still actively initiating people while promoting the practice of TM as pri-

marily a scientific technique and not as a religious act contrary to one's beliefs.

B. Is TM religious?

1. Before evangelism can occur, Christians must first recognize that the Bible condemns idolatry and that the practice of TM fits the Bible's description of idolatry.

2. Christians must then determine how this issue affects the views of the person who is considering being initiated, who is currently practicing TM, or who is a former meditator.

C. How is the practice of TM an act of idolatry?

1. What the Bible Has to Say about Idolatry

    a. When the Lord established the Ten Commandments for his chosen people, he said, "You shall have no other gods before me. You shall not make for yourself an idol in the form of anything in heaven above or on the earth beneath or in the waters below. You shall not bow down to them or worship them" (Exod. 20:3–5).

    b. The Lord also said, "Do not make any gods to be alongside me; do not make for yourselves gods of silver or gods of gold" (v. 23; see also Lev. 26:1), nor "make for yourselves an idol, an image of any shape, whether formed like a man or a woman . . . or like any creature. . . . do not be enticed into bowing down to them and worshiping [them]" (Deut. 4:16–19).

    c. The apostle Paul warned, "Therefore, my dear friends, flee from idolatry. . . . the sacrifices of pagans are offered to demons, not to God, and I do not want you to be participants with demons" (1 Cor. 10:14, 20).

2. TM's Initiatory Ceremony

    a. To practice TM, candidates must receive a *mantra,* a Sanskrit word or phrase, with which to meditate. The meditator repeatedly says the mantra in a relaxed, sitting position.

    b. To receive a TM mantra, candidates must participate in an initiation ritual.

    c. The candidates are requested to bring flowers, fruit, and a clean white handkerchief to the ceremony, where they are offered on an altar to an image of Guru Dev, Maharishi's deceased master.

    d. The TM instructor then praises Guru Dev as the embodiment of the Hindu *trimurti*—Brahma, Visnu, and Siva.

        (1) The candidates are ignorant of what is being sung because the invocation is in Sanskrit, and the TM instructor is required not to reveal the English translation to the ordinary initiate.

        (2) A part of the hymn is translated as follows: "GURU in the glory of BRAHMA, GURU in the glory of VISHNU, GURU in the glory

of the great LORD SHIVA, GURU in the glory of the personified transcendental fulness of BRAHMAN, to Him, to SHRI GURU DEV adorned with glory, I bow down."[1]

(3) The singing of this invocation is known as the *puja,* a Sanskrit hymn of worship, which is the heart of this initiatory ceremony.

e. The major purpose of the puja is to produce an altered state of consciousness in both the TM instructor who recites the puja and the candidates who hear it during the initiatory ceremony.

(1) Maharishi makes this clear in *The Holy Tradition,* which he gives to all TM instructors whom he has personally trained.

(2) Maharishi teaches that invoking the puja is so perfect that "the initiator's awareness is taken to the level of inner Being, then brought out to the relative in order to instruct the initiate. Through this instruction the initiate's awareness is led to the Absolute several times so that more and more of Its abundance is incorporated in his life."[2]

f. Even though the TM instructor assures concerned candidates that the puja is merely paying respect to Maharishi's honored tradition and that they are only passive observers, the candidates are actually actively involved in the puja ceremony.

(1) First, by bringing offerings that are given to Hindu divinities (required);

(2) Second, by taking off their shoes, smelling the incense, and bowing before Hindu images (which is optional);

(3) Finally, by later reciting their mantras, which in most cases are names of Hindu deities.

g. After the TM initiator instructs the initiates on how to pronounce their mantras, the initiator advises them to meditate on the mantra from fifteen to twenty minutes each morning and evening.

(1) Although TM instructors insist that these mantras are meaningless sounds with vibrational qualities that benefit the nervous system, others credit these mantras with spiritual powers.

(2) Hindu scholar Ludmilla Zielinski notes, "Traditionally, a mantra is a sacred text. . . . according to certain Hindu schools, the beginning of the world was an emanation of a Vedic word, or words, originally pronounced by Brahman and revealed to the Seers who recorded them for future generations. For that reason, these words are now holy and indestructible. When properly repeated by an initiate, a mantra can—according to

---

[1]This English translation is from the official TM version of *The Holy Tradition* (p. 5), a handbook Maharishi gives to TM teachers.

[2]Ibid., 6.

Hindu beliefs—produce miracles. . . . But [the initiate] must be initated first—and as a rule, by a guru who himself has already gained insight into the mystical power of the mantra."[3]

(3) In addition, "the mantra is an invocation to the Hindu god by that name. An Indian author, now turned Christian, the Reverend Douglas Shah, notes he has overheard the mantras of more than a dozen people and each have been the name of a Hindu god or goddess."[4]

D. What is the best way to evangelize those who practice TM?

1. What if the person who is considering being initiated into TM, or who is currently a TM meditator, or who used to be a meditator, professes to be a Christian?

   a. If the person truly is a Christian, then the material presented in II.C above should convince him or her that the Bible clearly condemns the initiatory ritual and practice of TM.

      (1) You can add this comment on Matthew 6:7 by David Haddon: "Jesus specifically rejected repetitive verbal exercises like mantramic meditation as means to God when he said, 'When you are praying, do not use meaningless repetition, as the Gentiles do [NASB].'"[5]

      (2) New religious movements researcher Marcia Greene says, "The Christian who takes [Scripture] seriously must reject Transcendental Meditation on all levels—in its practice and philosophy as well as its initiation ceremony."[6]

   b. If the person ignores the biblical verses cited in II.C above as well as Jesus' admonition in Matthew 6:7, then that person's theology is either weak or terribly flawed.

      (1) With some people who have recently become Christians, it takes a period of biblical study before they understand that certain behavior and beliefs are unacceptable to God. Thus mature Christians should gently and patiently instruct them in God's truths.

      (2) Other people, who profess to be Christians yet reject biblical instructions, can be cancerous to the life of a Christian community since they are likely to spread their false beliefs to other believers. Thus Christian leaders should firmly and lovingly confront and discipline these people.

---

[3]Ludmilla Zielinski, "Yoga, Meditation, Mantras," in *Maharishi: The Founder of Transcendental Meditation*, ed. Martin Ebon (New York: Signet Books, 1968), 117–18.

[4]Anonymous, "Can't be Catholic and practice TM," *Catholic Voice*, 17 November 1975, 4.

[5]David Haddon, "Transcendental Meditation," in *A Guide to Cults and New Religions*, ed. Ronald Enroth et al. (Downers Grove, Ill.: InterVarsity Press, 1983), 146.

[6]Marcia Greene, "From Religion to Science to Siddhis: The Evolution of the TM Movement," *Spiritual Counterfeits Project Journal* (Winter 1984): 61.

2. What if the person who is considering being initiated into TM, or who is currently a TM meditator, or who used to be a meditator, does not profess to be a Christian and has a low view of the Bible?

   a. Presenting the material in II.C above should not be the primary focus while evangelizing these people.

     (1) You might be able to convince them that the practice of TM *is* religious and that the TM organization is deceptive, but if they renounce this practice yet disregard Christ, nothing of eternal value is actually accomplished in God's eyes.

     (2) If, however, the person is led to the Lord, then the presentation of the material in II.C will be spiritually meaningful to him or her.

     (3) In other words, becoming a Christian must come first before persuading the person of the idolatrous nature inherent in the practice of TM.

   b. Nevertheless, there is value in discussing one feature of TM while sharing Christ with a non-Christian meditator.

     (1) TM would not interest most of these people unless they were seeking something to improve the quality of their lives.

     (2) TM's promise to provide inner peace is quite inviting to such people.

     (3) Even if a meditator experiences some form of stress relief or inner tranquility, it can be only transitory.

     (4) The point is that only Jesus can give true, eternal peace and rest: "Come to me, all you who are weary and burdened, and I will give you rest" (Matt. 11:28).

   c. At this point you can explain to your friend how Jesus cleanses us of sin and guilt, heals our broken relationship with God, strengthens our character so we can meet the daily challenges of life, and instills in us a certain hope for eternal glory in heavenly fellowship with him and God.

   d. Unlike TM's promises, Christ's promises provide true inner peace to those who devote their lives to him.

III. Western Adherents of Hinduism

A. Who are they?

1. Most of these people are primarily attracted to the experiential element of Eastern religions.

   a. Commenting on the 1993 Parliament of the World's Religions, I wrote, "These people were much like most Westerners who dabble in Eastern religions. They are far more interested in what they can mystically experience than what they can theologically understand."[7]

b. My observation was reinforced at a Parliament session where Yoga Guru, a modest, elderly "holy man" from India, tried to present his religious philosophy. After about ten minutes, one of his Western listeners interrupted him and led most of the attendees in chanting the sacred Hindu word OM for the rest of the session.

2. The practice of Yoga is not only a major component of Hinduism but also Hinduism's chief appeal to Westerners.

a. Yoga offers a wide variety of spiritual experiences.

b. The following groups popular in North America teach various systems of yoga (defined here or below) to their devotees: Maharishi and his TM organizations teach Raja Yoga; ISKCON (Hare Krishna movement) teaches Bhakti Yoga; Swami Satchidananda and his Integral Yoga Institute teach Hatha Yoga; the Ananda Marga Yoga Society teaches Karma Yoga; Satya Sai Baba's foundation teaches Siddha Yoga (tantric power yoga); and Yogi Bhajan and the 3HO teach Kundalini Yoga (serpent power yoga).

B. What is yoga?

1. *Yoga* is a Sanskrit term that literally means "discipline"; it is a derivative of *yuj*, which means "to yoke" or " to concentrate the mind."

2. Yoga comprises numerous theoretical and technical systems for doing Eastern meditation.

a. Although yoga is taught in some Buddhist and Jaina schools, it is primarily associated with the Hindu tradition.

b. The purpose of all methods of yoga is to transform human awareness into pure consciousness—that is, liberation from discrimination while attaining undifferentiated union with the primal essence of consciousness.

c. A guru (a spiritually accomplished teacher) must initiate and instruct the spiritual seeker because yogic disciplines are not easily learned.

3. The exact origin of yoga is uncertain.

a. The first evidence of yoga appears in the Upanisads.[8]

b. In perhaps the third or fourth century A.D., Patanjali compiled the classical *Yogasutra,* which became the core text of the yoga traditions.

c. Tantric rituals and philosophy had a profound effect on yoga.

(1) Tantric literature commenced sometime between A.D. 300 and 600.

---

[7]J. Isamu Yamamoto, "The Buddha and What He Taught," *Christian Research Journal* (Spring–Summer 1994): 34.

[8]See Maitri Upanisad 6.18.

(2) Tantrism is a shamanistic religion whose quest is to control supernatural forces to accelerate one's spiritual development and enhance one's spiritual powers.

(3) "While orthodox Hindus view occult powers as impediments to the quest for *moksa* [liberation from rebirth and suffering], tantrics court them as proofs of progress. The orthodox view a temperate life-style as essential to the pursuit of Yoga, but tantrics cultivate the sensuous elements in their psychic makeup.... Hindu tantric texts are a distinct, less respected, and often censured corpus."[9]

(4) Nevertheless, syncretism occurred between tantrism and some schools of yoga that have developed into separate systems of yoga, which have become immensely popular in the West.

d. Major systems of yoga[10]

(1) *Jnana Yoga,* the discipline of knowledge; attaining *moksa* through reflective meditation.

(2) *Karma Yoga,* the discipline of action; ethical conduct that does not produce karmic results.

(3) *Bhakti Yoga,* the discipline of devotion; devotion of one's life and actions to a particular god, such as Krisna, Rama, or Siva.

(4) *Mantra Yoga,* the discipline of audition; repeating sacred sounds (mantra) formed from Sanskrit letters in order to attain supernatural powers and esoteric knowledge.

(5) *Laya Yoga,* the discipline of dissolution; constant meditation on the divine lord (Isvara) who symbolizes the oneness of all things.

(6) *Hatha Yoga,* the discipline of exertion; comprehensive control over the body through prescribed postures, breath exercises, and rigorous diet.

(7) *Raja Yoga,* the discipline of the classical way; study of Patanjali's *Yogasutra* while mastering various meditation techniques to achieve *samadhi*—absolute independence of one's soul, self, or consciousness (*purusa*) from the material world (*prakrti*).

C. **What is wrong with yoga?**

1. Yoga is highly visible in American society.

a. Yoga is taught in public schools, business workshops, and community centers.

b. Yoga is featured on daily television programs.

---

[9]A. Bharati, "Tantrism," in *The Perennial Dictionary of World Religions,* ed. Keith Crum (San Francisco: Harper Collins, 1989), 735.

[10]G. J. Larson, "Yoga," in *The Perennial Dictionary of World Religions,* 815.

   c. Books and periodicals on yoga line the shelves in major bookstores and public libraries.

   d. Celebrities, educators, and politicians credit yoga for enriching their lives and improving their health.

2. The public perception of yoga is that it is a regimen for physical conditioning whose religious roots can be ignored.

   a. The most common system of yoga employed for physical exercise is hatha yoga.

   b. Yet even hatha yoga is deeply rooted in Hindu philosophy. David Fetcho says, "The fact remains that even physical yoga is inextricably bound up in the whole of Eastern religious metaphysics. In fact, it is accurate to say that physical yoga and Indian metaphysics are mutually interdependent; you really can't have one without the other."[11]

   c. Moreover, Fetcho says, "yoga postures are themselves specifically designed to manipulate consciousness . . . and move the mind into raja yoga's consummate experience of *samadhi*."[12]

   d. Although Western practitioners of hatha yoga claim that this technique is simply another aid to physical fitness, "the techniques of *hatha* are given to prepare a person's consciousness for the subtler metaphysics of *raja* yoga."[13]

   e. French scholar Alain Danielou says, "The sole purpose of the physical practices of Hatha Yoga is to suppress physical obstacles on the spiritual and Royal path of Raja yoga: and Hatha yoga is therefore called 'the ladder to Raja yoga.'"[14]

3. Thus it does not matter what system of yoga is taught; its very nature is interdependent with the doctrines and spiritual experiences associated with Hindu philosophy.

D. What is the best way to evangelize those who practice yoga?

1. If the people involved with yoga are Christians, a clear explanation of what yoga is should steer them away from it. (Otherwise, consult II.D.1 above.)

2. If the people are non-Christians who are merely dabbling with yoga, a clear presentation of the gospel is more important than challenging the benefits or the metaphysical nature of yoga. (For additional suggestions, see II.D.2 above.)

---

[11]David Fetcho, *Hatha Yoga: Simply Physical Exercise?* (Berkeley, Calif.: Spiritual Counterfeits Project, 1982), 1. Fetcho is cofounder of the Spiritual Counterfeits Project and a former member of the Ananda Marga Yoga Society.

[12]Ibid.

[13]Ibid., 2.

[14]Alain Danielou, *Yoga: The Method of Re-Integration* (New York: University Books, 1955), 17.

3. If the people are Western adherents to Hinduism, a basic understanding of Hindu philosophy and terms is necessary in order to discuss intelligently their search for ultimate truth.

   a. Although people value mystical experience over rhetorical logic while discussing religious doctrines, it is important to have some idea of what they are talking about when they use such common Hindu terms as *karma, samsara, samadhi,* and *yoga.*

   b. Christians can dismiss the assertion that the central teachings of Hinduism and Christianity are in harmony by being prepared with biblical statements that contradict Hindu teachings.

   c. Thus the adherents of Hinduism are left with the choice of either continuing on the Hindu path or turning to Jesus as the only way to God, no longer being able to believe that divergent spiritual journeys is not a crucial issue.

4. Since American adherents of Hinduism place an exalted premium on what they experience when they practice yoga, Christians must try to show that an experience in itself is neither self-validating nor trustworthy in perceiving truth.

   a. First, when they speak of their mystical experiences, their description of those experiences is already a record of past experiences, and because those experiences are past—and they regard truth as ever evolving—their mystical experiences cannot be the basis of what they claim is present truth.

   b. Second, if they refer to Hindu philosophy to support their contention that their mystical experiences are a vehicle that leads to enlightened truth, they are not merely contradicting themselves but also violating their own assertion that yogic experiences are self-illuminating independent of philosophical dogma.

   It is important to take this argument one step further because they view "contradiction" as the illusory perception of the unenlightened.

   c. Third, their personal experiences are an attempt to realize and be absorbed in the impersonal Absolute.

      (1) Like the raindrop (Atman) becoming one with the cosmic ocean (Brahman), they seek to lose the identity of their souls in the Universal Soul. Simply put, it is a quest for self-annihilation.

      (2) At this point Christians should persuade these people not to continue to persist in a depersonalizing belief system and tug at their inner need for *personal* meaning toward a *personal* God who validates each person as an individual who is loved and forgiven by him through the *personal* sacrifice of his Son, Jesus Christ.

IV. Hare Krishna Devotees

A. Their Identity

1. Although the Hare Krishna movement in North America has always attracted only a small number of followers, the International Society for Krishna Consciousness (ISKCON) has received wide coverage from the Western press over the past three decades, particularly from the late 1960s to the early 1980s.

   a. Currently there are only a few thousand members of ISKCON in North America.

   b. Even at its peak, the Hare Krishna movement never grew beyond ten thousand full-time monks in the United States.

2. Most of the devotees in ISKCON have similar sociological backgrounds.

   a. They are usually white and from middle-class families.

   b. Most of them were in their twenties when they joined the movement.

   c. Those who rise into leadership roles have had some kind of higher education.

   d. They are primarily attracted to the communal life of this religious group and the total devotion to a personal god (that is, Krisna).

3. Although Krishna devotees frequently used to be seen at airports and in major city parks, asking for donations and selling their literature, for the most part they have withdrawn from the media spotlight.

   a. They still chant publicly while dressed in traditional Indian garments.

   b. They do this to express their unbridled love for and dedication to Krisna rather than to attract media attention.

B. Devotion to Krisna

1. Krishna devotees seek a transcendental love for and relationship with Krisna.

   a. They regard Krisna as a personal deity who lives in the heart of every human being.

   b. They believe that when they completely surrender themselves in devotion to Krisna, they attain true bliss and personal salvation.

   c. They also believe that the constant chanting of Krisna's name will not only enhance their love for Krisna but also achieve both temporal and ultimate union with him.

2. They view Prabhupada, the founder of ISKCON, as a mediator between Krisna and themselves.

   a. They consider their deceased master an incarnation of Visnu and of a higher spiritual level than Brahman and Siva.

    b. They also regard Prabhupada to be on a higher level than Christ is in the divine hierarchy.

C. *Common Ground*

  1. Both Christians and Krishna devotees can find common ground in their respective faiths in Christ and Krisna.

    a. By looking at similarities, Christians and devotees in most cases will avoid unnecessary arguments and establish some trust between them.

    b. Thus communication will become easier, and differences between the two faiths can be addressed, arriving at deeper insights for both parties.

  2. Both Christians and Krishna devotees believe in a god who is a personal savior.

    a. Unlike many Hindu monists, Krishna devotees recognize the need for a personal relationship with a deity-lord.

    b. "Hence, we have two gods who can be compared and contrasted, rather than two religious philosophies to be debated."[15]

  3. In addition, both Christianity and Krishnaism place considerable significance on the human heart.

    a. Thus the needs of the human spirit can be more readily mentioned and discussed.

    b. Most importantly, the common yearning to know and fellowship with a Supreme Being can be shared between Christians and Krishna devotees.

  4. Other areas of agreement include total commitment to a religious cause, the communion of believers, regular worship, and dedication to holy scriptures.

D. *Evangelistic Suggestions*

  1. Since the Bible is a source of spiritual inspiration and instruction for Krishna devotees, it is generally easier to use the Bible as a divinely authoritative document in discussing the person and work of Jesus Christ than it is with members of other Hindu groups.

    a. Nevertheless, while discussing the primacy of Christ, you may find that devotees will dispute the Bible's authority, but this response would be inconsistent with the teachings of their leaders, who commend the Bible as Holy Scripture.

    b. If they concede the authority of the Bible, then God's Word will play a key role in establishing the credentials of Jesus Christ.

    c. The major difficulty, however, is correcting the way they interpret Scripture. Moreover, devotees are taught not to engage in philosophical speculation.

---

[15]J. Isamu Yamamoto, "Hare Krishna (ISKCON)," in Enroth, *A Guide to Cults and New Religions,* 100.

    d. That is why Christians need to be grounded in God's Word and then keep the focus of their conversation with devotees on the personal significance of Jesus' atoning work for each believer.

    e. Though Christians don't have to be biblical scholars, they should obey the apostle Paul's instruction: "Do your best to present yourself to God as one approved, a workman who does not need to be ashamed and who correctly handles the word of truth. . . . And the Lord's servant must not quarrel; instead, he must be kind to everyone, able to teach, not resentful. Those who oppose him he must gently instruct, in the hope that God will grant them repentance leading them to a knowledge of the truth" (2 Tim. 2:15, 24–25).

2. Devotees within the ISKCON organization revere Jesus and his teachings.

    a. Krishna devotees will agree with Christians that everyone is a sinner, but they believe Krisna is their personal savior.

    b. Once the fact that sin has affected everyone is established, Christ and Krisna can be contrasted in order to testify to Christ as the only true redeemer (Heb. 10:10).

    c. The following questions can then be discussed: Can there be more than one savior? If so, why did Jesus say that he was the only way to the heavenly Father (John 14:6)? Why revere him if he made this claim? If not, who is the savior?

    d. A critical biblical passage should then be discussed: "Then know this, . . . It is by the name of Jesus Christ of Nazareth, whom you crucified but whom God raised from the dead, . . . Salvation is found in no one else, for there is no other name under heaven given to men by which we must be saved" (Acts 4:10, 12).

    e. At this point they must choose to pour out their love and devotion to either Krisna or Christ as their personal savior. Do they want inner bliss in Krisna or eternal joy in Christ?

V. Asian Indians in the United States

A. *Their Identity*

1. This ethnic group comprises Asian-Indian immigrants and Asian-Indian, American-born citizens.

    a. Together they presently number over 700,000 people.

    b. Their presence in North American society is growing dramatically.

2. This group of people is the most important in trying to understand because most Christians will encounter members of this group far more often than members of any of the three groups previously mentioned.

    a. Asian Indians and Asian-Indian Americans live in our neighborhoods.

    b. They attend the same classes we attend from primary school to the university.

    c. They work side by side with us no matter what occupation we are in.

    d. They often attend to our medical needs.

    e. They serve us when we do our banking and shopping.

    f. Most importantly, many of them are our friends.

B. Assimilation into American Society

  1. Most Asian Indians who come to North America are fluent in at least three languages.

    a. They learn their regional mother tongue while growing up.

    b. They must study English throughout their schooling because the texts are in English.

    c. They are taught Hindi, the Indian national language, from the sixth grade through high school.

    d. They are required to learn another language in high school, with many studying Sanskrit for several years.

    e. Some also can converse in other regional dialects.

  2. Most Asian-Indian Americans are not as proficient in languages as Asian-Indian immigrants, but they are still multilingual.

    a. English is their primary language.

    b. They usually pick up their parents' mother language in the home for conversing.

    c. They can also study Hindi, Sanskrit, and other Indian languages, which may be taught at the local temple.

  3. The majority of Asian Indians living in the United States are highly educated.[16]

    a. 52 percent of all Asian Indians in the United States over the age of twenty-five are college graduates (compared with only 16.2 for the U.S. population as a whole).

    b. 30,000 are physicians or medical professionals.

    c. 45,000 are engineers.

    d. 25,000 are scientists and professors.

    e. 3,000 are in law, finance, and business.

C. Religious and Cultural Distinctives

  1. Although many Asian Indians are affiliated with Sikhism, Islam, or Christianity, most Asian Indians belong to the Hindu religion.

    a. Since Hinduism is a noninstitutional religion, much of the Hindu religious life of Asian Indians is private.

---

[16]Statistical data is from Richard A. K. Shankar, "Asian Indian Americans," in *Encyclopedia of Multiculturalism,* ed. Susan Auerbach (New York: Marshall Cavendish, 1994), 1:214.

b. In many Hindu households, a small area is designated as a shrine for daily prayers. Each shrine contains pictures and miniature statues of deities for whom incense and an oil lamp are lit and for whom prayers are said each morning and evening.

c. Asian Indians are constructing more and more Hindu temples, which serve as centers for Hindu cultural and religious life.

2. Although this is less the case with their American children, Asian Indian immigrants seek to preserve their cultural identity.

   a. They will not eat beef or bovine products because they believe cows are sacred animals in their Hindu belief system.

     (1) Many will not eat any kind of meat, including fowl and fish, because they do not believe in the taking of life.

     (2) Instead of demanding that their children not eat meat for religious reasons, many parents try to persuade them to refrain for health reasons.

   b. Besides language and diet, many Asian Indians, especially women, wear traditional Indian clothing most, if not all, of the time.

     (1) This is not the case, however, with their children and younger Asian Indians.

     (2) Yet on special religious occasions they will observe the Indian dress code.

   c. Asian Indians want their children to marry within their own ethnic group.

     (1) While the majority of Asian Indians insist that their children marry other Hindu Asian Indians, the rest would prefer that they do.

     (2) Those who "prefer" actually are more concerned about their children's staying within their own ethnic group rather than marrying outside their religious faith.

D. Evangelistic Suggestions

1. Christians need to be aware of the sociological differences between Asian-Indian groups.

   a. Marked cultural differences exist between people from North India and people from South India.

     (1) Asian Indians from North India tend to be more traditional, have male-dominated families, and venture into small businesses.

     (2) Asian Indians from South India are more academically trained and in the professional fields, and their women are more educated.

     (3) Whereas Asian Indians from North India might resist the gospel because of cultural reasons, those from South India might use liberal, theological arguments to dismiss the gospel.

(4) Thus Christians should find out the cultural background of Asian Indian friends to discover how best to present the gospel.

   b. Christians also need to understand that not all Asian Indians belong to the Hindu faith.

(1) Many Asian Indians are Muslims, Sikhs, and even Christians, each faith having its own traditions and belief system.

(2) Although Hinduism is primarily an Indian religion, Christians must be careful not to offend Asian Indians by assuming they are Hindus and classifying all under one religious faith.

2. Asian Indians do not perceive a difference between various "Christian" groups.

   a. They view Mormons and Jehovah Witnesses as being of the same faith as evangelical Christians.

(1) Since many Hindus disdain the aggressive evangelism of these cults, they automatically close their minds when evangelicals try to share the gospel with them.

(2) Even when Christians try to explain the theological differences between Christian orthodoxy and cults, Asian Indians are likely to regard the differences as merely a result of sectarian conflicts among Christian groups.

(3) Therefore Christians should address those issues that pertain to who Christ is and what he has accomplished as the distinguishing point between groups claiming to be Christian.

   b. Many Asian-Indian Hindus naturally believe that Hinduism is intellectually and culturally superior to Christianity.

(1) They are offended when Christians seek to explain the Christian faith but lack any desire to learn about their own or, worse yet, have preconceived ideas that reflect badly on their native religion and culture.

(2) For example, it would be a terrible blunder to associate their religion with the Hare Krishna movement, TM, or even Sai Baba.

(3) Having some understanding of Hindu philosophy will not only help Christians articulate the gospel in a way that their Hindu friends will understand the Good News about Christ but also encourage those friends to be more willing to listen.

(4) In addition, Hindus see the moral corruption in the West and conclude that Christianity has failed to better the human race.

(5) Instead of pointing out the evils in Indian society, Christians should reflect the godly character of Christ and credit Christ for those virtues their Asian-Indian friends see in them, thus affirming the gospel message they have shared with their friends.

 Part IV:
Selected Bibliography

I. Primary Sources of Hinduism

A. Sruti ("that which is heard")

The Vedas.

> The four Vedas comprise *Rg Veda, Yajur Veda, Sama Veda,* and *Atharva Veda.* Each includes Samhitas (poems and hymns), Brahmanas (ritualistic precepts and sacrificial duties), and Aranyakas (philosophical commentary).

The Upanisads.

> On the one hand, the Upanisads are the fourth part of each of the four Vedas; on the other hand, the Upanisads are a major departure from the religious view of the Brahmanas with a strong emphasis on spiritual monism in which truth is discovered through intuition rather than reason.

B. Smrtis ("that which is remembered")

Ramayana

> This Indian epic describes the exploits of Rama, an avatar (incarnation) of the god Visnu.

Mahabharata

> This sacred epic relates the stories of the descendants of Bharata and focuses on the teachings of Krisna, another avatar of Visnu.

Bhagavad-Gita

> This discourse between Krisna and Arjuna, his friend, is actually a section of the *Mahabharata*; yet it is one of the most authoritative texts in Hinduism.

Puranas

> These sacred texts are a collection of Indian myths and legends that are primarily concerned with the three major Hindu gods—Brahma (as the creator), Visnu (as the preserver), and Siva (the destroyer).

Sutras

> These systematic treatises formed the doctrines of the major schools of modern Hinduism.

Sastras

> These writings, the most important being *Laws of Manu,* comprise legal and ethical instructions.

II. Secondary Sources of Hinduism

A. *Major Comprehensive Works*

Crum, Keith, ed. *The Perennial Dictionary of World Religions.* San Francisco: Harper & Row, 1989.

This dictionary was originally published as *Abingdon Dictionary of Living Religions* (1981). It is an outstanding reference source that clearly and accurately defines all the basic concepts of the Far Eastern Religions.

Dasgupta, Surendranath. *A History of Indian Philosophy.* 5 vols. Cambridge: Cambridge University Press, 1922–69.

An exhaustive study of Hinduism, examining its evolution, sacred texts, and varied manifestations in India.

Noss, David S., and John B. Noss. *Man's Religions.* 7th ed. New York: Macmillan, 1980.

This standard reference book covers the history of all the major religions as well as many of the minor ones.

B. *Major Books on Hinduism*

Dimmitt, Cornelia, and J. A. B. van Buitenen. *Classical Hindu Mythology: A Reader in the Sanskrit Puranas.* Philadelphia: Temple University Press, 1978.

This anthology contains lucid translations of these Hindu myths as well as insightful explanations of their sources.

Dumont, Louis. *Homo Hierarchicus: The Caste System and Its Implications.* Chicago: University of Chicago Press, 1980.

Dumont's cogent examination of the Indian caste system is a major contribution to understanding the religious doctrines that support it.

Edwards, Paul. *Reincarnation: A Critical Appraisal.* Amherst, N.Y.: Prometheus Books, 1996.

Edwards provides astute arguments against the logic of reincarnation.

Hopkins, Thomas J. *The Religious Life of Man: The Hindu Religious Tradition.* Belmont, Calif.: Wadsworth, 1971.

Hopkins's book is still an exceptional study of the development of Hindu philosophy.

Kramrisch, Stella. *The Presence of Siva.* Princeton, N.J.: Princeton University Press, 1981.

Kramrisch's examination of the Hindu scriptures pertaining to the Hindu god Siva is erudite and thorough.

O'Flaherty, Wendy Doniger. *The Origins of Evil in Hindu Mythology.* Berkeley, Calif.: University of California Press, 1980.

O'Flaherty's work is a fascinating exploration of the Hindu perception of evil.

_____. *Siva: The Erotic Ascetic.* Oxford: Oxford University Press, 1973.

This book analysizes the paradoxical characteristics of Siva and his powerful influence over those devoted to him.

Radhakrishnan, Sarvepalli. *Religion and Society.* London: George Allen & Unwin, 1959.

"Widely regarded as the most brilliant of India's modern intellectuals,"[1] Radhakrishnan (1888–1975) presents this modern classic on Hinduism.

Radhakrishnan, Sarvepalli, and Charles A. Moore, eds. *A Sourcebook in Indian Philosophy.* Princeton: N.J.: Princeton University Press, 1957.

This indispensable compilation of significant passages from sacred Hindu texts provides an illuminating understanding and explanation of Hindu thought from its beginning over four thousand years ago.

Yogananda, Paramahansa. *Autobiography of a Yogi.* Los Angeles: Self-Realization Fellowship, 1972.

This autobiography of one of Indian's most charismatic holy men has had profound influence on Western seekers fascinated with Eastern mysticism.

Zaehner, R. C. *Hinduism.* London: Oxford University Press, 1966.

Zaehner's book is a first-rate introduction to the basic elements of Hinduism.

_____, ed. *Hindu Scriptures.* London: Everyman's Library, 1966.

A collection of key Hindu scriptures that include the Vedas, Upanisads, and Bhagavad-Gita while providing the number for each verse, which is important in locating specific statements and citation.

III. Christian Discussions of Hinduism

A. Major Books

Albrecht, Mark. *Reincarnation: A Christian Critique of a New Age Doctrine.* Rev. ed. Downers Grove, Ill.: InterVarsity Press, 1987.

Albrecht examines not only the doctrinal tenets of reincarnation as an Indian teaching but also its recent impact on Western society, and he cogently argues how it conflicts with biblical teaching.

Beaver, R. Pierce, et al. *Eerdmans' Handbook to the World's Religions.* Grand Rapids: Eerdmans, 1982.

For a fine introduction to Hindu philosophy, see Raymond Hammer's "The Eternal Teaching: Hinduism," 170–72; "Roots: The Development of Hindu Religion," 173–84; "Concepts of Hinduism," 185–92; and "Hindu Worship and the Festivals," 193–95.

---

[1]James F. Lewis and William G. Travis, *Religious Traditions of the World* (Grand Rapids: Zondervan, 1991), 292.

Enroth, Ronald, et al. *A Guide to Cults and New Religions*. Downers Grove, Ill: InterVarsity Press, 1983.

This collection of essays, which focuses on the most publicized new religious groups to emerge in the West in the past three decades, includes revealing looks at the Hare Krisna movement and Transcendental Meditation.

Halverson, Dean C., ed. *The Compact Guide to World Religions*. Minneapolis: Bethany House, 1996.

This book provides a helpful overview of the major features of Hinduism with excellent charts and tips on how to share one's Christian faith with Hindus.

Johnson, David L. *A Reasoned Look at Asian Religions*. Minneapolis: Bethany House, 1985.

Johnson presents an insightful analysis of the major schools of Hindu thought.

Lewis, James F., and William G. Travis. *Religious Traditions of the World*. Grand Rapids: Zondervan, 1991.

This scholarly work offers a clear and comprehensive understanding of the history and religious doctrines of India.

Maharaj, Rabindranath, with Dave Hunt. *Death of a Guru*. New York: A. J. Holman, 1977.

This inspiring biography of a prominent Hindu who became a dedicated follower of Jesus Christ offers invaluable insights in the field of missions and evangelism.

Sire, James W. *The Universe Next Door*. 2d ed. Downers Grove, Ill.: InterVarsity Press, 1988.

Sire's classic, which explores modern worldviews, includes a perceptive chapter on Eastern pantheistic monism, a dominant strand of classical Hinduism.

B. *Major Journals*

Spiritual Counterfeits Project Journal

This journal includes several articles that focus on different aspects of modern Hinduism.

Albrecht, Mark. "World Views in Contrast." (Winter 1984): 38.

Alexander, Brooks. "Shamanism in Two Cultures: Tantric Yoga in India and Tibet." (Winter 1984): 29–30.

_____. "Occult Philosophy and Mystical Experience." (Winter 1984): 13–19.

Greene, Marcia. "From Religion to Science to Siddhis: The Evolution of the TM Movement." (Winter 1984): 55–61.

Christian Research Journal

These issues of the journal cover current and significant events pertaining to Hinduism in America.

Miller, Elliot. "Parliament of the World's Religions: Part I: Interreligious Dialogue or New Age Rally?" (Fall 1993): 8–15.

_____. "Parliament of the World's Religions: Part II: The Fundamentalism of Tolerance." (Winter 1994): 16–19, 32–35.

Rabey, Steve. "Maharishi, Inc." (Winter 1997): 48–49.

Part V:
Parallel Comparison Chart

Hinduism, TM and Hare Krishna	The Bible

History

"The four Ages known as Krta, Treta, Dvapara and Kali comprise 12,000 divine years [equal to about 4,320,000 human years during one cycle of these Ages]" (Markandeya Purana 43).

"In the Kali Age [present evil age], men will be afflicted by old age, disease, and hunger.... Then the Age will change, deluding their minds like a dream, by the force of fate, and when the Golden Age begins, those left over from the Kali Age will be the progenitors of the Golden Age.... Thus there is eternal continuity from Age to Age" (Linga Purana 1.40.72–83).

"In the beginning, O Lord, you laid the foundations of the earth, and the heavens are the work of your hands. They will perish.... But you remain the same, and your years will never end" (Heb. 1:10–12).

"Jesus Christ is the same yesterday and today and forever" (Heb. 13:8).

"Then I saw a new heaven and a new earth, for the first heaven and the first earth passed away.... There will be no more death or mourning or crying or pain, for the old order of things has passed away" (Rev. 21:1, 4).

Absolute Truth

"Those sinners who have constantly condemned Vedas, gods or brahmins, those who have ignored the beneficial teachings of Purana and Itihasa ... all these fall into these hells" (Vamana Purana 12.1).

"Hinduism has no fixed creed by which it may be said to stand or fall, for it is convinced that the spirit will outgrow the creed. For the Hindu every religion is true, if only its adherents sincerely and honestly follow

"Have nothing to do with godless myths" (1 Tim. 4:7).

"I am not ashamed of the gospel, because it is the power of God for the salvation of everyone who believes" (Rom. 1:16).

Jesus said, "I tell you the truth, until heaven and earth disappear, not the smallest letter, not the least stroke of a pen, will by any means disappear from the Law until everything is accomplished" (Matt. 5:18).

82

Absolute Truth (cont.)

it" (Radhakrishnan, *Religion and Society*, 53).

"Religion should not be confused with fixed intellectual conceptions, which are all mind-made. Any religion which claims finality and absoluteness desires to impose its own opinions on the rest of the world" (Radhakrishnan, *Religion and Society*, 52).

"Grace and truth came through Jesus Christ. No one has ever seen God, but God the One and Only, who is at the Father's side, has made him known" (John 1:17–18).

"I have not spoken in secret, from somewhere in a land of darkness; I have not said to Jacob's descendants, 'Seek me in vain.' I, the LORD, speak the truth; I declare what is right" (Isa. 45:19).

"Jesus answered, 'I am the way and the truth and the life. No one comes to the Father except through me'" (John 14:6).

Salvation of the Soul

"He who in fancy forms desires, because of his desires is born [again] here and there" (Mundaka Upanisad 3.2.2).

"The early Christian church accepted the doctrine of reincarnation.... The truth is that man reincarnates on earth until he has consciously regained his status as a son of God" (Yogananda, *Autobiography of a Yogi*, 199).

"When the dweller in the body has overcome the gunas [essence of nature] that cause this body, then he is made free from birth and death, from pain and decay: He becomes immortal" (Bhagavad-Gita 14.20).

"There can be no real perfection for us except by our inner self" (Aurobindo, *The Life Divine*, 931).

"As [Jesus] went along, he saw a man blind from birth. His disciples asked him, 'Rabbi, who sinned, this man or his parents, that he was born blind?' 'Neither this man nor his parents,' said Jesus" (John 9:1–3).

"Just as man is destined to die once, and after that to face judgment, so Christ was sacrificed once to take away the sins of many people" (Heb. 9:27–28).

Jesus said, "For my Father's will is that everyone who looks to the Son and believes in him shall have eternal life, and I will raise him up at the last day" (John 6:40).

"By one sacrifice [Christ] has made perfect forever those who are being made holy" (Heb. 10:14).

Salvation of the Soul (cont.)

"When a Yogin pronounces the syllable OM, it reaches the crown of his head. When a Yogin is absorbed in the syllable OM, he becomes eternal.... He becomes one with Brahman.... He wins absorption in Brahman, in the supreme ultimate Self" (Markandeya Purana 39.6, 16).

Jesus said, "For God so loved the world that he gave his one and only Son, that whoever believes in him shall not perish but have eternal life.... Whoever believes in the Son has eternal life, but whoever rejects the Son will not see life, for God's wrath remains on him" (John 3:16, 36).

Jesus Christ

"I don't think Christ ever suffered or Christ could suffer.... It's a pity that Christ is talked of in terms of suffering" (Yogi, *Meditations of Maharishi Mahesh Yogi*, 123–24).

"No man on earth has ever maintained spiritual poise all through his life. The Jesus who declared that men must not resist evil if they are to become the sons of the Father who makes his sun shine upon good men and bad, and his rain to fall upon the just and the unjust, was the same Jesus who cursed the fig-tree and drove the tradesmen from the temple" (Radhakrishnan, *A Sourcebook in Indian Philosophy*, 634).

"The great masters of India mold their lives by the same godly ideals that animated Jesus.... Freemen all, lords of themselves, the Yogi-Christs of India are part of the immortal fraternity" (Yogananda, *Autobiography of a Yogi*, 195–96).

"[Jesus] said to them, 'How foolish you are, and how slow of heart to believe all that the prophets have spoken! Did not the Christ have to suffer these things and then enter his glory?' " (Luke 24:25–26).

"Therefore, since we have a great high priest who has gone through the heavens, Jesus the Son of God, let us hold firmly to the faith we profess. For we do not have a high priest who is unable to sympathize with our weaknesses, but we have one who has been tempted in every way, just as we are—yet was without sin" (Heb. 4:14–15).

"[Christ] committed no sin, and no deceit was found in his mouth" (1 Peter 2:22).

"But you know that [Christ] appeared so that he might take away our sins. And in him is no sin" (1 John 3:5).

Jesus warned, "Watch out that no one deceives you. For many will come in my name, claiming, 'I am the Christ,' and will deceive many" (Matt. 24:4–5).

Jesus Christ (cont.)

"Whoso in Man knows Brahman, knows the highest Lord. . . . Whereas the gods who Brahman know revere Brahman as the highest, best" (Atharva Veda 10.7.17, 24).

"Therefore God exalted him to the highest place and gave him the name that is above every name, that at the name of Jesus every knee should bow, in heaven and on earth and under the earth, and every tongue confess that Jesus Christ is Lord, to the glory of God the Father" (Phil. 2:9–11).

God

"That the gods ever may be with us for our gain, our guardians day by day unceasing in their care. May the auspicious favour of the gods be ours, on us descend the bounty of the righteous gods. The friendship of the gods have we devoutly sought; so may the gods extend our life that we may live" (Rg Veda 1.89.1–2).

"In the beginning this [universe] was Brahman alone. . . . So, whoever reveres any other deity, thinking: 'He is one, and I am another,' does not [rightly] understand" (Brhadaranyaka Upanisad 1.4.10).

Lord Krisna declared, "Know that all beings have their birth in this. I am the origin of all this world and its dissolution as well. There is nothing whatever that is higher than I. . . . I am the syllable Aum [OM] in all the Vedas. . . . I am not in them [all beings]; they are in Me" (Bhagavad-Gita 7.6–8, 12).

"They become the ocean itself. . . . Whatever they are in this world, whether tiger, or lion, or wolf, or boar, or worm, or fly, or gnat, or mosquito, that they become. That which is the

"Acknowledge and take to heart this day that the LORD is God in heaven above and on the earth below. There is no other" (Deut. 4:39).

"'You are my witnesses,' declares the LORD, 'and my servant whom I have chosen, so that you may know and believe me and understand that I am he. Before me no god was formed, nor will there be one after me'" (Isa. 43:10).

"In the beginning God created the heavens and the earth" (Gen. 1:1).

The God of Israel said, "I am the LORD, and there is no other; apart from me there is no God. . . . It is I who made the earth and created mankind upon it. . . . And there is no God apart from me, a righteous God and a Savior; there is none but me. . . . I am God, and there is no other; I am God, and there is none like me" (Isa. 45:5, 12, 21; 46:9).

"God said to Moses, 'I AM WHO I AM. This is what you are to say to the Israelites, "I AM has sent me"'" (Exod. 3:14).

God (cont.)

finest essence—this whole world has that as its self. That is Reality. That is *Atman.* That art thou, Svetaketu" (Chandogya Upanisad 6.10.1–3).

"He who finds his happiness within, his joy within, and likewise his light only within, that yogin becomes divine" (Bhagavad-Gita 5.24).

"Hear, O Israel: The LORD our God, the LORD is one" (Deut. 6:4).

"'The most important [commandment],' answered Jesus, 'is this: "Hear, O Israel, the Lord our God, the Lord is one"'" (Mark 12:29).

 **Part VI:**
Glossary

The small "u" is pronounced as in *cut*.

Advaita (ud-VI-tu) A doctrine that affirms that reality is nondualistic.

Ahimsa (u-HIM-sa) The absence of the desire to kill or injure another living being, or not wishing to harm others.

Ananda (a-NUN-du) Bliss or pure joy.

Asanas (A-su-nus) Bodily postures required during the practice of yoga; it means "to sit quietly."

Asrama (ASH-ru-mu) The four stages of life of a devout Hindu, comprising (1) student (Brahmacarin); (2) householder (Grhastha); (3) forest-dweller (Vanaprastha); and (4) renouncer (Sannyasin).

Atman (AT-mun) The eternal soul of a living being that seeks union with the Universal Soul (Brahman).

Avatar (A-vu-tar) An incarnation of a god, particularly Visnu, into a human being or animal; this concept is absent in the Vedas and Upanisads and is first introduced in the Bhagavad-Gita.

Bhagavad-Gita (BU-gu-vud-Ge-tu) A section of the Hindu epic Mahabharata in which Lord Krishna discourses with Arjuna about the true nature of ultimate reality, providing the dominant themes of Hindu philosophy; the words mean "song of the glorious one."

Bhakti (BUK-te) The devotional system of yoga, involving worship of personal deities.

Brahma (BRA-ma) The creator deity in the Hindu pantheon.

Brahman (BRU-mun) The Universal Soul; the ultimate reality; the chief god in the Hindu pantheon; supreme holy power; class of priests and preservers of the Vedic doctrine; the highest caste among Hindus (commonly referred to as "Brahmins").

Brahmanas (BRAH-mu-nus) Vedic texts that provide instructions for performing sacrifices to the deities.

Darsana (DAR-shu-nu) Any Indian philosophical view of truth—in particular those attempts to gain liberation (*moksa*) from the cycle of rebirths (*samsara*); a few schools like the *Carvaka*, however, dismiss the idea of liberation; the meaning of this term is "seeing."

Dharma	(DAR-mu) Laws governing the natural order, which includes ethical precepts.
Dhyana	(di-A-nu) Meditation during the practice of yoga.
Guru	(goo-roo) A spiritual teacher; the term means "to lift up."
Karma	(KAR-mu) The ethical and physical consequences of human actions, which also affect future existences.
Krisna	(KRISH-na) A human incarnation of the Hindu god, Visnu; Visnu's eighth avatar; one of the most popular deities in India.
Linga	(LING-u) Sign of the male sex organ; especially symbolic of the phallus of the Hindu god Siva.
Mantra	(MUN-tru) A verbal formula or hymn, usually in Sanskrit, which a person repeats during meditation to invoke the presence of a particular divinity.
Maya	(MA-ya) The ability of supernatural beings to assume material form and exert extraordinary powers over humans; a false dualistic perception of true reality that results from ignorance of the oneness of all things.
Moksa	(MOK-shu) Mystical liberation when a Hindu becomes one with the Universal Soul (Brahman) and is released from the cycle of birth and death.
Nirvana	(nir-VA-nu) The result of enlightenment in which one's individual self becomes one with ultimate reality (which is to be distinguished from the Buddhist definition in which one's personal identity is "extinguished").
OM	(om) The supreme Vedic syllable, used as a mantra to evoke the primal powers of Brahman; it means "yes, so be it."
Prajna	(pruj-NYA) Intuitive wisdom in which one comes to true knowledge of the way things are.
Prakrti	(PRA-kri-te) The manifestation of Brahman in material form, in contrast with purusa.
Purusa	(poo-ROO-sha) The manifestation of Brahman as consciousness, in contrast with prakrti.
Puja	(POO-ja) The ritual presentation of offerings, service, and homage to honor someone, typically performed for a Hindu god before its image at an altar.
Rishi	(RI-she) Seer or sage; one who has knowledge.
Samadhi	(su-MA-di) Intense concentration in order to attain the cessation of mental activity.
Samsara	(sum-SA-ru) The transmigration of the soul from one living being to another through successive lives.

Sannyasin (sun-YA-sin) A Hindu who has renounced the world and is free from all attachments and desires, seeking only *moksa* (final liberation).

Sanskrit (SAN-skrit) Sacred language of Hinduism; considered the language of the gods; the language of the Aryans who invaded India in the second millennium B.C. and the language of the Vedas.

Siddhi (SID-de) Attainment of supernatural psychic powers while practicing yoga.

Smrti (SMRI-te) Hindu religious texts written after the Vedas; the term means "that which is remembered"; they include the Ramayana, Mahabharata (with the Bhagavad-Gita), Sutras, and so on; with the exception of the Bhagavad-Gita, this body of religious works is not as highly esteemed as the Vedas and Upanisads.

Sruti (SHROO-te) Hindu scripture that comprise the Vedas and Upanisads; the term means "that which is heard"; Hindus believe the gods directly imparted this wisdom to the ancient sages, and therefore these texts are the most sacred and authoritative of Hindu literature.

Trimurti (tri-MUR-te) The trimorphic god in three forms as Brahma (the creator), Visnu (Vishnu—the preserver), and Siva (Shiva—the destroyer).

Upanisad (oo-PUN-i-shud) The last of the four writings to each of the four Vedas, and which means "to sit near to"; they comprise exchanges between a teacher and student in which monistic philosophy is asserted.

Vedas (VA-dus) Sacred knowledge transmitted through special revelations from god to holy men and composed into hymns, ritual texts, and philosophic discourses.

Yoga (YO-gu) A physical or mental discipline whose purpose is to take the adept from self-awareness to pure consciousness; it is a vehicle to release one from all discriminations.

Yuga (YOO-ga) An age or period of time; according to the Hindu tradition there are four yugas: Krta Yuga, Treta Yuga, Dvapara Yuga, and Kali Yuga, which occur and recur in a cyclical pattern; although the Vedas refer to the yugas, it wasn't until the Puranas and Epics that they became systematized.

Zondervan Guide to Cults and Religious Movements
TRUTH AND ERROR
by Alan W. Gomes

Softcover 0-310-22049-1

Truth and Error provides the parallel comparison charts that are featured in all the books included in the Zondervan Guide to Cults and Religious Movements. These charts offer a quick reference to the main theological issues of each religious group and their differences with Christianity. This book is a guide and introduction to the entire series.

Zondervan Guide to Cults and Religious Movements are affordable books that provide a concise introduction, a theological overview, witnessing tips, a bibliography, and a comparison chart that shows the essential differences between Christianity and the cult group. These user-friendly books are top quality because each is written by a different author who is an expert on the specific cult or religious group.

Fast, informed answers to the challenges of false religions!

Available at your local Christian bookstore.

ZondervanPublishingHouse
Grand Rapids, Michigan
http://www.zondervan.com

Zondervan Guide to Cults and Religious Movements
JEHOVAH'S WITNESSES
by Robert M. Bowman Jr.
Softcover 0-310-70411-1

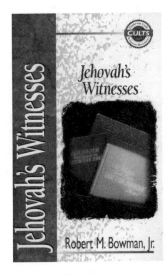

Here's how you can more clearly dialog with people from other religious groups who come knocking on your door. The Zondervan Guide to Cults and Religious Movements book on Jehovah's Witnesses will provide you with the answers you need. This book details the history and theology of the Jehovah's Witnesses and gives you witnessing tips for reaching out to their members with the Gospel of Christ.

Zondervan Guide to Cults and Religious Movements are affordable books that provide a concise introduction, a theological overview, witnessing tips, a bibliography, and a comparison chart that shows the essential differences between Christianity and the cult group. These user-friendly books are top quality because each is written by a different author who is an expert on the specific cult or religious group.

Fast, informed answers to the challenges of false religions!

Available at your local Christian bookstore.

ZondervanPublishingHouse
Grand Rapids, Michigan
http://www.zondervan.com

We want to hear from you. Please send your comments about this book
to us in care of the address below. Thank you.

ZondervanPublishingHouse
Grand Rapids, Michigan 49530
http://www.zondervan.com